"This witty, immediately applicable, and action-oriented guide teaches that managing can be fun, meaningful, easier, and more peaceful."

—**David Bach, #1 *New York Times* bestselling author of *The Automatic Millionaire* and *Start Late, Finish Rich***

"Don't let the laughter fool you. In here there is very serious and insightful guidance on how you can get out of others' (and your own) way so everyone can excel. There are plenty of useful examples and practical tips to please even the most obsessive-compulsive types."

—**Jim Kouzes, coauthor of the bestseller *The Leadership Challenge***

"Why do so many managers hate managing? Devora Zack tackles that question head-on in a book that should be on every manager's reading list. Zack identifies skills and techniques that will help you manage authentically—and effectively."

—**Tony Bingham, President and CEO, American Society for Training and Development**

"Like the author, this book has bounce and sass, plus great ideas and examples. If you want to retain your talented employees, read this book—cover to cover!"

—**Beverly Kaye, coauthor of *Help Them Grow or Watch Them Go***

"Zack's sparkling personality bursts from the pages to guide readers in a delightful and entertaining way."

—**Amy Lemon, Volunteer Management, Smithsonian Institution**

"Zack's insight and her engaging writing style make this book easy to read and fun to apply in your business and personal life."

—**Hector Vargas, Managing Director, Training Solutions, Mexico and Central America**

"Management is as much an art as it is a science. Zack provides insights on the importance of both and practical advice on how to improve performance."

—**Jerome E. Hass, Professor Emeritus of Finance and Business Strategy, Johnson Graduate School of Management, Cornell University**

"This book is a life-saver for any managers who woke up one day to discover they're suddenly in charge."

—**Rachel Lam, Senior Vice President and Group Managing Director, Time Warner Investments**

"My manager was so inept, his boss sent him to a Myers-Briggs class, and another participant told him he was a first-class J-E-R-K! If he'd read this book, he would have learned why he was ineffective and how to successfully capitalize on his gifts! Delightful and insightful!"

—**Chip R. Bell, coauthor of *Wired and Dangerous***

"Leaders and managers often have to deal with the elephant in the room—or worse, being the elephant in the room. This book shows how to do it properly."
—Jeff Weirens, Principal, Deloitte Consulting LLP

"Zack's entertaining and accessible guide to building management skills is essential for new managers and pretty damn useful for old ones as well."
—Patrick L. Phillips, CEO, Urban Land Institute

"Management is a profession that leaves really smart people scratching their heads and hoping for a miracle. At last that miracle is here."
—Vivienne Anthon, FAIM, CEO, Australian Institute of Management, Queensland, Australia

"I laughed, I sighed, I went right out and bought three more copies of this lighthearted yet heavy-on-wisdom book for my favorite managers."
—Elaine Biech, author of *Training for Dummies* and *The Business of Consulting*

"Read this book! You'll thank me later."
—Jules Polonetsky, former Senior Vice President, AOL

"I couldn't put this book down! Zack boils down the wisdom of dozens of management tomes, teaching how to match your personality and management style. As entertaining as it is effective!"
—Howard Wiener, Principal, KPMG

"Like a stress-relieving lunch with your best friend at an outdoor café Devora demonstrates she feels your pain, gives you hope, and shares secrets to get real results."
—Grant D. Marques, Vice President, Global Business Services, CSC

"For managers seeking an effective, personalized style of leadership, Zack's book is a perfect guide."
—Dr. Hubert Lobnig, faculty, University of Klagenfurt, Austria

"Learn to effectively manage your team and—miraculously—have fun doing it."
—Jeff Cooke, Manager, John Deere

"Zack's tested methods and tailored advice enable all personality types to hone their management styles and find the recipe for success."
—Barbara Rosenbaum, Vice President, Capgemini Government Solutions

"Bravo! This book provides you with all the tools, strategies, and tricks nobody ever told you you'd need in management."
—Meredith Pierce Hunter, Director, Alumni Relations, London Business School

Managing for People Who Hate Managing

We're our own dragons as well as
our own heroes, and we have to
rescue ourselves from ourselves.
—Tom Robbins,
  Still Life with Woodpecker

BY DEVORA ZACK

Managing for People Who Hate Managing:

BE A SUCCESS
BY BEING YOURSELF

ILLUSTRATIONS BY
JEEVAN SIVASUBRAMANIAM

Berrett–Koehler Publishers, Inc.
San Francisco
a BK Business book

Berrett-Koehler Publishers, Inc.
235 Montgomery Street, Suite 650
San Francisco, CA 94104-2916
Tel: (415) 288-0260   Fax: (415) 362-2512   www.bkconnection.com

ORDERING INFORMATION

Quantity sales. Special discounts are available on quantity purchases by corporations, associations, and others. For details, contact the "Special Sales Department" at the Berrett-Koehler address above.

Individual sales. Berrett-Koehler publications are available through most bookstores. They can also be ordered directly from Berrett-Koehler: Tel: (800) 929-2929; Fax: (802) 864-7626; www.bkconnection.com

Orders for college textbook/course adoption use. Please contact Berrett-Koehler: Tel: (800) 929-2929; Fax: (802) 864-7626.

Orders by U.S. trade bookstores and wholesalers. Please contact Ingram Publisher Services, Tel: (800) 509-4887; Fax: (800) 838-1149; E-mail: customer.service@ingrampublisherservices.com; or visit www.ingrampublisherservices.com/Ordering for details about electronic ordering.

Berrett-Koehler and the BK logo are registered trademarks of Berrett-Koehler Publishers, Inc.

Printed in the United States of America

Berrett-Koehler books are printed on long-lasting acid-free paper. When it is available, we choose paper that has been manufactured by environmentally responsible processes. These may include using trees grown in sustainable forests, incorporating recycled paper, minimizing chlorine in bleaching, or recycling the energy produced at the paper mill.

Library of Congress Cataloging-in-Publication Data

Zack, Devora.
    Managing for people who hate managing : be a success by being yourself/ by Devora Zack ; illustrations by Jeevan Sivasubramaniam.
— 1st ed.
        p. cm.
    Includes bibliographical references and index.
    ISBN 978-1-60994-573-2 (pbk.)
    1. Executive ability. 2. Executives—Psychology. 3.—Psychological aspects. I. Title.
    HD38.2.Z335 2012
    658.4'09—dc23   2012025980

First Edition
17 16 15 14 13 12   10 9 8 7 6 5 4 3 2 1

Designed and produced by Seventeenth Street Studios
Illustrations by Jeevan Sivasubramaniam with Jeremy Sullivan
Copy editing by Todd Manza, Manza Editorial
Cover/jacket Design by Susan Malikowski, DesignLeaf Studio.
Cover photography by Bob Elsdale Photography Ltd.

For

. . . you

Contents

Welcome to the Electrifying World of Management

The only way to do great work is to love what you do.

—Steve Jobs

People crave success.

Success of all kinds. Particularly their own. Definitions of achievement vary madly, yet success in many, many professions comes with a caveat: As you rise upward in your field you also—more likely than not—become

a manager!

Congratulations.

Now, get to it. There are performance evaluations to deliver, people to reprimand, forms to fill out, crowds to address, protocol to follow, feedback to provide, staff to hire, others to fire, meetings to run, communication to bungle, projects to lead, teams to inspire, direct reports to herd, expectations to fulfill, apologies to make, priorities to clash, programs to off-load, correspondence to correct, names to memorize, meetings to blow off, subordinates to appease, plus hours and hours and hours to work late.

And always have a smile on your face or people will talk. *Make sure it's authentic.*

Oh, and do your real job, too.

Did I mention your training will be minimal to none? And your every move will be scrutinized, judged, and dissected ad nauseam? Starting . . . now!

What are you standing around for? Get busy. Run. RUN!

Wait! Get back here. Take this book with you. You'll need it.

CHAPTER ONE

Why You Hate It, Why I Wrote This

Find a job you like and you add five days to every week.
—H. Jackson Brown, Jr.

So much to do in every day
Never wanted to manage anyway
Just do your work and what I say
So my last nerve doesn't fray.

Hey!

I'm so glad you stopped by. Our expedition navigating the crazy, stormy waters of Managing People will be well worth the time you devote. Plus, reading this book may count as professional development. You go!

On these pages you'll find heaps of useful, lifesaving management tips. Euros well spent, if you ask me. Consider this book a leadership life vest, only more flattering. Your being here makes the whole insane process of writing worthwhile. In fact, I wrote this book for you (see the dedication).

You Have Questions, I Have Answers

Before we delve in, a few pesky questions are pounding at the door, demanding our attention.

WHY DOES THIS BOOK EXIST?

As a management consultant for more years than is really your business, I've seen plenty of fads come and go. I could list them here to make my point, except that would be criminally tedious. Plus, my up-and-coming readers will have no idea what I'm talking about. That's the point: Fads go. Splitsville. Ta-ta. Heartlessly leaving us panting in the very offices where they sought us out, promised the world . . . then promptly turned on their heels following the big gala thrown in their honor.

There are way beyond plenty of management books out there. Why didn't I choose to write about an underrepresented topic in business literature? The impact of solar eclipses on manager tirade cycles, for example.

I'm focusing on this topic because it is so stinkin' essential. Learning techniques to reverse your secret hatred of managing can have a colossal impact on your work life—to infinity and beyond. We are teetering on the verge of a veritable management big bang.

Notice I said "reverse your secret hatred" not "how to deal with people even though you can't stand managing them."

Our aim is to discover a method of managing that you don't hate. The reason you won't hate it is because it fits who you are.

Managing isn't just something we do while walking purposefully in big buildings with lots of windows. Management is about communication, rapport, morale, and productivity. For starters.

WHAT IS MANAGING, ANYWAY?

Aah, the bazillion dollar question. I'll take an IOU.

Any half-baked MBA knows that we could argue all day about the truest, bestest definition of *manager.* Didactics bore me, however. So let's put our heads together and think about the brass tacks of what we expect in a quality manager (precluding, for now, the rest of your job, such as whittling widgets or multiplying money). What does managing boil down to?

Managing is the high-wire act of balancing useful guidance and getting out of the way.

If you got to handpick a person to manage you, wouldn't you tag someone with a variation of the above recipe?

Providing useful guidance presupposes that a manager has the requisite ability and credentials. Equally essential is having the wherewithal to know when to step aside to let others grow, excel, and mess up. When in doubt, pour a higher proportion of letting-others-shine into your management protein shake. (Chapter 7 delves into this.)

WHY DO PEOPLE HATE MANAGING?

A startling percentage of us dislike, even (shh!) hate managing. What is the source of this international travesty? Much managerial angst springs from two causes.

1. You pursue a career of interest. You turn out to be halfway decent at it, earning a promotion. Suddenly, you find yourself in the alarming, distressing quandary of Managing People. You have less time to do what stimulates you and more responsibility for motivating, leading, and prodding others.

2. Let's not mince words. Managing others can be a real buzz kill. You gotta deal with all their . . . stuff. When did you wake up and suddenly become a therapist, mediator, and cruise director?

In a nutshell, we want to do what we consider our *real* work; managing gets in the way.

Management is not your passion; your real job is.

And that, my friends, is the elephant in the room. (You knew that was coming; may as well get it over with early on). A recent Berrett-Koehler study of 150 leaders from nearly as many industries revealed that only 43 percent are comfortable being managers, with a mere 32 percent saying they like being managers.

Translation, anyone? Too subtle a statistic? Allow me to spell things out.

Chances are less than one in three that your manager is amused to be managing you. Depending on your own little idiosyncrasies, the actual percentage could be even more skewed against you! Yet I'm certain that is not the case.

Help is on the way. Legions of managers suffer needlessly from the misperception that to be a *real* manager they must somehow assume a plethora of traits that don't come close to seeming natural. Plus, they believe real managers don't eat quiche. This is untrue and smacks of prejudice against egg farmers.

I say, stop the madness!

The reverse is true. The only way to achieve success as a manager —and to garner the rewards and benefits of managing—is to lead from a place that is authentic to your core. Frittatas all around.

Because most normal people spend the majority of their waking hours preoccupied with vital matters other than personality functioning, knowing oneself can get shoved to the side. Unhelpfully, a startling number of business books direct you to look outside yourself for clues on how to manage the masses. This book, instead, crystalizes your understanding of hot-ticket items such as:

- What is your natural management style?
- How do you make decisions?
- What are your strongest traits?

- Do you lead from your head or your heart?

- How can you figure out what matters most to people on your team?

- What's the best way to reinforce positive behavior?

- How can you leverage your strengths to manage others?

... and the biggie ...

- How can you be both true to yourself and flexible in how you manage others?

The answers to these questions add up to the Uniquely You formula for brilliant management. No, it is not a hair coloring.

WHY IS THIS BOOK ACTION-PACKED?

Down with passivity! People learn through involvement. My favorite Chinese proverb puts it succinctly:

"Tell me and I'll forget. Show me and I may remember. Involve me and I'll understand."

Action is particularly important to book readers. Have you ever read a book and thought it quite good . . . then couldn't recall a single tangible thread six months later? I am determined to fight this trend. The best way to reap sustainable benefits from a book is through your active involvement in the escapade.

Recall seeing a "Save the _____!" ad and thinking, "Wow! That's a really important cause! I'm going to make a donation." If you don't do it on the spot, chances are zip to nil you ever will. Here are a couple of reasons why.

1. We forget within forty-eight hours half of what we hear and learn.

2. We are most likely to convert intention into reality by taking action close to the point of inspiration.

That's why merely providing instructions on, say, How to Manage Better yields low retention and weak results. You won't remember what you read . . . or the changes you were temporarily inspired to make. Relevant examples to demonstrate techniques help. Actively engaging readers while they are reading—through activities, assessments, and exercises—enables new skills to really take hold.

Because different styles capitalize on unique strengths, this book kicks things off with an easy-to-take, versatile assessment in chapter 2, "Who Are You?" Then you get to jump through a few hoops. You'll find segments throughout the book called "Jumpin' Thru Hoops." These are your opportunity to apply ideas to your own journey. You don't get to just sit and read. You have to stay awake and alert, with a zillion opportunities (with a margin of error ± 3) to convert content into relevant action.

What more could you want out of life? Real-life examples? You got it. "Sample Examples" are scattered like breadcrumbs marking your way through the forest. You also will come across boxes called "On a Related Note," with tidbits related to the primary chapter themes.

Even if everything else around you collapses to bits, we'll always have fond memories of traipsing through this book together.

WILL I EVER ACHIEVE MY LOFTY AMBITION OF A ONE-WORD BOOK TITLE?

I saved the most critical question for last. Please arrange a write-in campaign to my editors. I need all the momentum I can get on this failed campaign.

Two Tales

Tatiana was a marvelous, motivated manager at an international organization headquartered in Washington, DC. Upon her promotion to management, Tatiana inherited a handful of a team. Her direct reports were impressively opinionated, outspoken, cynical, and authority adverse. True to form, the team was instantly skeptical of Tatiana as their new manager. I use the term *team* loosely, because this crew was more invested in coalitions and gossip than in team building. To heighten the situation, many had held the same position for over a decade while somehow dodging any meaningful feedback or real accountability.

Tatiana meant business. She was as eager to build productivity as she was to create rapport, with neither goal particularly prized by her dozen direct reports. Tatiana's office was a few floors above her team, in a sprawling office building, emphasizing her heightened role and presumed distance from the commoners. This rank-based arrangement made Tatiana uncomfortable, so she made a point of hand delivering the mail (which arrived first at her office) to her staff's desks three floors down. Standard operating procedure was for supervisors to e-mail staff and let them collect mail and other pertinent paperwork themselves. Tatiana intended to demonstrate camaraderie and respect by making the trek herself. This was typical of Tatiana's style; her actions and choices reflected her natural humility.

What did the team think about her mail delivery service? They were livid. Their new manager was intolerable! Evidently, she neither respected nor trusted them. And how did they arrive at this rock solid conclusion?

"She spies on us!" they proclaimed. "Instead of calling us into her office to get our mail, she brings it down here as an excuse to sneak up on us." That was all the data they required to prove their theory. Case closed.

Momentarily file away that story and follow me across the globe to the open bush of Australia.

Upon my arrival in Australia for a speaking tour, I was invited on an excursion around the area surrounding Queensland's lovely coastal town of Maroochydore. Shortly into the bus ride, the driver, Paul, a dedicated local, pointed far into the bush where he spotted a roo (Aussie for kangaroo). I desperately wanted to see my first wild roo and strained to search the landscape. To my consternation, my unaccustomed eyes couldn't distinguish roo from bush.

Upon the tour's conclusion, Paul asked how I'd liked everything. I thanked him for his top-notch job introducing us to his beloved countryside yet admitted disappointment in missing the roo. An expert in catastrophic thinking, I was certain I'd bungled my one and only chance in this lifetime to view a real roo.

Paul reassured me, "I think we can arrange a viewing for you." He instructed me to stay on board while the others disembarked, and then we drove a short distance to the University of Southern Queensland, where seventy or eighty wild roos roamed free on the campus. Immediately upon our arrival we spotted two glorious specimens in plain view, basking in the sun rays. I was wild with excitement.

"Can I crawl out there and pet one?" I asked, ridiculously.

"Sure, mate," he replied in laid-back Aussie style.

On hands and knees, I crawled stealthily (at least that's how I like to recall it) into the bush. I strategically made a wide arc around the roos and, remaining unnoticed, positioned myself immediately behind them. Dizzy with success, I reached out a hand to touch the larger one on her back.

I somehow failed to notice that the smaller roo was apparently an offspring, whom the mother was obliged to protect. The plot thickens.

The mom roo had not expected me to suddenly appear behind her, and she was startled. She jumped up on her back legs, whirled to face me, assumed boxing position, and prepared for battle. Far off in the distance, I heard my guide say in his steady voice, "Now crawl away . . . quickly."

I managed to emerge unscathed. I did nothing, however, toward advancing my relationship with roos.

Naturally, this brings us to the question of why so many managers harbor a strong dislike for managing. Tatiana and the roos intersect to illustrate the mysterious Big Mess commonly referenced as Managing.

The following comparisons are provided for your consideration.

Scenario	Deliver the Mail	Pet the Roo
Intentions of Tatiana and me	To form a positive bond	To form a positive bond
Behaviors of Tatiana and me	Humble, active gesture to demonstrate respect for the team	Quiet, low, soft approach to demonstrate peaceful intention
Desires of team and roo	To be left alone	To be left alone
Interpretation by team and roo	DANGER! Space violation	DANGER! Space violation
Inner reaction of team and roo	Threatening situation!	Threatening situation!
Outer reaction of team and roo	Prepare for battle	Prepare for battle

How are complete disconnects between intentions and interpretations possible? Are these the only two examples of this kind or— more alarmingly—are they everywhere, permeating the very fabric of our existence?

I'd prefer to not answer that question. Yet I will, out of sheer commitment to your professional success. Typical interplay between intention and interpretation:

Yes, gentle reader. These disconnects permeate the very fabric of our existence. There. I said it. Best to get things out in the open at the start of a relationship, don't you think? So you know what you're getting yourself into. For those of you who want to exit the book now, I understand. Just remember, you can run but you can't hide. Nice meeting you.

For those of you who stuck around, I'm glad you don't succumb to panic easily.

Let's Get It Started

A journey of a thousand steps (not so bad, given inflation these days) starts with understanding your own sweet self. Luckily, I've done the heavy lifting for you. All you need to do is grab a latte, relax at a swank café, and hold up this book for onlookers to jot down the title.

Reading an e-book? Curses! Foiled again.

To recap: People hate managing because it's draining and interferes with addressing substantial other demands on their time. Plus there's

On a Related Note

The [yawn] Leadership–Management–Supervision Debate

In some circles, *manager* is a bad word. "Managers manage and leaders lead" is proclaimed definitively—sand in the face of people who naively use the inferior term *manager*. Then there are supervisors. What a mess! With so many of these leaders, managers, and supervisors wandering around, how can anyone get any work done? It's all so overwhelming.

Presumably leaders have vision. (I don't. I've worn glasses since the age of seven.) Supervisors, on the other hand, oversee, say, a factory assembly line. And managers hit a snag midway through their careers, caught in the tumbleweeds of telling others what to do on a daily basis. Heated, theoretical arguments take place over the jostling stature accompanying each title.

This is a bunch of baloney. In the real world, where staff meetings are held and paychecks are distributed every other week, terminology is irrelevant. What matters is how people are treated. They don't care if you supervise, lead, or manage them. They care whether you've got their back, whether you are invested in their success, and whether you treat them as assets, liabilities, or competition.

I defer to other authors in moving along this riveting debate.

a misconception that you have to smash your personality into a pre-defined mold to be a good manager (and land that coveted VIP parking space).

This book helps you discover a leadership style perfectly suited to you, capitalizing on your natural strengths. As a result, managing becomes easier and more enjoyable.

You'll learn how to be a top-notch manager, being true to yourself while adapting to honor the preferences of others. By the way, having an adaptive style doesn't mean letting people off the hook. It means understanding how others perceive reality and working within that construct for mutual success. The first step is clarifying your own style. Interested?

Join me at the next chapter.

CHAPTER TWO

Who Are You?

But enough about me, let's talk about you . . . What do you think of me?
—C. C. Bloom (Bette Midler's character in *Beaches*,
screenplay by Mary Agnes Donoghue)

There once was a manager named You
Who had no idea what to do
Until You took this here quiz
Took control of your biz
Into a leadership star You grew.

Why don't managers just read a well-respected tome on Management (there are several options available with that very title!), do as instructed, and move on with their lives?

Because there is not one correct way to do things. There are endless variables that factor into how to manage most effectively, and they differ with every single person on your team.

If that isn't an exhausting thought, I don't know what is.

People come equipped with this pesky item commonly referred to as a Personality. Personalities are infuriating. Particularly when yours differs from mine. Once we get to know each other, yours can be intolerable even when it is quite similar to mine, just to keep things jumping. In fact, I can hardly stand my own half the time.

When are those robot people predicted back in the 1970s going to emerge?

As an MBA, I am trained to resort to Useful Charts and Numbers to make a point. Here's mine:

Me (manager) + You (staffer) = **Ka-Boom!**

Part of the confusion and general chaos lurking just a millimeter behind the surface of any basic, seemingly well-functioning organization is due to cataclysmic clashes of personality.

There are many aspects to personality. Thinker–Feeler is one of four dimensions highlighted in the Myers–Briggs Type Indicator and is linked to how we make decisions, communicate, and manage. To satisfy the curiosity of the academics out there, MBTI has roots in the teachings of Carl Jung. Think of Jung as the grandfather of personality theory. Maybe great-grandfather by now.

Managing for People Who Hate Managing (MFPWHM. Such a catchy acronym . . . so memorable!) will guide you through the Thinker–Feeler continuum, a sublime cavern of our inner worlds. You will learn versatile techniques to be a stellar manager by being yourself. You on board?

The good news keeps on coming. The techniques introduced are transferable to virtually all management situations. I don't even know why I said "virtually." I can't think of any exceptions. With all those lawyers out there, you can't be too careful. If you discover an exception, e-mail my people. I will claim it didn't make it to my desk.

Let's start with the basic premise everybody thinks and everybody feels. Well, nearly everyone, but that's an issue we'll deal with later. For our current purposes, this premise works.

Managers are in the position to make gobs of decisions daily. Quickly. How you make decisions is a key aspect of how you manage. Notice I didn't say *what* decisions you make. We're a layer deeper than that here . . . digging down into the *way* you make decisions.

Although thinkers are (for the most part) capable of actual feelings, and feelers (despite misconceptions) really do think.

Thinkers lead with their heads; feelers lead with their hearts.

From this page forward, when we say "thinker" (or just T), that is shorthand for "people who primarily think to make decisions." And when we say "feeler" (or just F), what we're really saying is "people who primarily feel to make decisions."

This chapter also discusses the continuum of thinkers and feelers, because there are gradations, levels, degrees, if you will.

The Royal Rule

It's insane to assert there are hard-and-fast rules for being the best of all managers. A real sickness. Okay, so there is *one* rule. And *I* get to set it. Cue fanfare!

The only indisputable, irrefutable, inarguable, brilliant, life-changing rule, doctrine, law, MANDATORY realize-it-or-regret-it foundation of being the best possible manager ever is:

... be you.

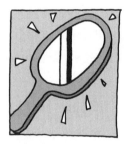

Piece of cake, no? Perhaps a complex, homemade, multistep, carefully executed, and years-to-develop cake recipe. Maybe that.

There are a startling number of steps and skills involved in being yourself. Sigh. Is *nothing* easy in this world? My sentiments precisely.

Luckily, I've thrown away years of a potentially lighthearted, carefree life to benefit you.

While you were doing . . . whatever . . . I've had my nose to the grindstone, focused almost exclusively on the nuances of personality. Sure, I come up for air and regular feedings, but that's about it. And now, with minimal exertion on your part, I am handing my findings over for your consumption and daily use. Start thinking about a meaningful holiday gift now; it's never too early.

The path toward *being* you is *knowing* you. The upcoming assessment pinpoints a key aspect of your personality, helping you harness the best you have to offer as a manager.

The Thinker–Feeler continuum (we will also reference it as T/F) is a prime indicator of how one manages in a work environment. This preference affects both behavior and internal processing of experiences.

You'll learn about different personality types—not just your own but also others, because you are undoubtedly managing plenty of lunatics from "the other side" (that is, whichever side is not your own). Understanding people's behavior at work will reduce your frustration and increase your efficiency. This frees up your time and energy.

In case you are wondering, personality temperaments are innate. That means your preference, your essence, your natural style, is part of your core. This does not limit you in any way. You are in charge of your abilities—and can teach yourself whatever skills you deem important. Plenty of people become so adept at modeling behaviors from an opposite temperament that the casual observer would believe it's their natural style. This is not being artificial; it is being *flexible*. Lots more on this ahead.

Now, tighten that safety belt across your lap—we're about to reveal the *Real You* beneath that suave exterior. It's high time.

SELF-ASSESSMENT INSTRUCTIONS

Each numbered item offers two options to complete a sentence. Assign three points between these two options based on your natural preferences and point of view. Point distributions are 3 and 0, or 2 and 1, no half points. If you agree entirely with A and not at all with B, assign A = 3 and B = 0. If you relate somewhat with A yet more with B, assign A = 1 and B = 2. Respond based on your natural temperament, not learned behavior or what you think is "right."

1.	**A top manager displays:**	
	A. Strength and analysis	1
	B. Empathy and concern	2
2.	**It is more important to:**	
	A. Learn and use people's names	2
	B. Promote logically and consistently	1
3.	**Teams work best when:**	
	A. Participants feel safe and respected	2
	B. Participants have clearly defined roles	1
4.	**Before hiring someone, I:**	
	A. Check references and education	1
	B. Must feel a rapport and connection	2
5.	**When giving feedback, I:**	
	A. Want the other person to feel heard	2
	B. Focus on what needs to change	1
6.	**If laying off an employee, my primary concern would be:**	
	A. Ensuring my documentation is in hand	2
	B. His or her personal, emotional reaction	1
7.	**Employees work hardest when they believe:**	
	A. They are making a meaningful contribution	3
	B. The company is solvent and well structured	0
8.	**To motivate others, I:**	
	A. Provide regular positive reinforcement	3
	B. Provide performance improvement strategies	0
9.	**I assess my management skills by whether I:**	
	A. Strengthen and develop technical skills	1
	B. Strengthen and develop confidence and relationships	2
10.	**A key to good leadership is:**	
	A. Authority	1
	B. Empathy	2

11.	**If I am reasonably certain my path will not cross someone else's again:**	
	A. I still care about having a positive interchange	2
	B. I don't much care whether they like me or not	1
12.	**I am more pleased with a day that:**	
	A. I am super efficient	2
	B. I make someone's day with a kind act	1

Self-Assessment Scorecard

(Be alert! Columns include a mix of A and B!)

1.	A =	1	B =	2
2.	B =	1	A =	2
3.	B =	1	A =	2
4.	A =	1	B =	2
5.	B =	1	A =	2
6.	A =	2	B =	1
7.	B =	0	A =	3
8.	B =	0	A =	3
9.	A =	1	B =	2
10.	A =	1	B =	2
11.	B =	1	A =	2
12.	A =	2	B =	1
Totals (36)	Thinker =	12	Feeler =	24

32–36: Strong preference

28–31: Clear preference

22–27: Moderate preference

19–21: Slight preference

The Spectrum

All personality dimensions exist along a continuum. There are not two paper-cutout versions of personalities, pure thinkers (T) or pure feelers (F). If only! Imagine how much easier staff meetings would be—particularly if the two camps held separate meetings.

There are a slew of styles. T/F is one of many different aspects of our complex dispositions. Other personality dimensions influence our interactions as well. For example, introversion and extroversion also play into management style, as addressed in chapter 9. However, this book highlights T/F because of its uniquely strong, direct impact on how we manage.

To keep things lively, Ts and Fs come equipped with nuances. Along the way, you'll meet Ts and Fs with strong, clear, moderate, or slight preferences. What I call an off-the-chart T (preference rating 32–36) is notably different from a slight T (preference rating 19–21). Nevertheless, we gain tremendous insight even by focusing broadly on the distinguishing traits of Ts and Fs.

What if you are in the middle? Let's say you scored a dead heat of 18/18 on the assessment—or real close to it. Do you need immediate treatment? No. Scoring in or near the middle of the continuum does not correlate with being flaky, wishy-washy, or confused. Instead, your results indicate you have a solid dose of both thinker and feeler attributes inside of you. You are good to go.

Scoring a tie or slight preference indicates you can understand, relate to, and manage a range of personalities with less effort than those of us entrenched in the distant ends of the spectrum. Looking in my crystal ball, I'd say you also come equipped with a natural ability to establish rapport, build coalitions, and mediate conflict. Others can learn these skills, too. It just comes more easily for you. At the same time, it is certainly useful to gain a solid understanding of those who exhibit stronger preferences than yourself.

While keeping in mind variations among Ts and Fs, we will pay the most attention to the outer ends of the continuum. This is done intentionally, to clarify differences. We need to understand what distinguishes thinker and feeler management styles to become attuned to more subtle distinctions.

Feelers & Thinkers

There's a reason for everything, even for titling this section "Feelers & Thinkers" rather than "Thinkers & Feelers": the Fs would read into it if they were listed second and the Ts couldn't care less. This is an example of how understanding different types sensitizes you to their needs and preferences.

If that's not something to look forward to, frankly, I don't know what is.

When introducing the T/F assessment, I'm often privy to protest. *Thinking* and *feeling* are loaded descriptors, and no one exists in an all-or-nothing situation.

This might be a shocker; prepare yourself. The T/F dimension is not linked to intellect. Or emotion. It also is not related to decisiveness or even the quality or outcomes of decisions. It has nothing to do with creativity. So what is T/F all about?

Your placement on the T/F continuum indicates whether you primarily lead with your head or with your heart. When deciding what to do in a situation, Ts consider principles and are typically drawn to the most rational choice, whereas Fs consider values and are often drawn to the most sensitive choice.

I prefer "Feeler" tendencies but maybe I think people expect or value "Thinkers" more?

Peruse this handy, portable summary sheet, created for your exclusive use:

Thinker managers are:
- Analytical
- Impartial
- Objective

Thinkers make decisions by going into thought.

Thinkers value:
- Logic
- Reason
- Justice

Thinkers separate emotions from goals and consequences.

Feeler managers are:
- Appreciative
- Involved
- Subjective

Feelers make decisions by going into feeling.

Feelers value:
- Harmony
- Kindness
- Empathy

Feelers identify with and assume others' emotional states.

You *can't* make everyone happy, a fact that makes Ts shrug and Fs sob in despair (at least internally). However, you *can* assess a situation and notice your natural response. Take a reality check by discussing and calibrating your reactions with others. Consider the best overall outcome and adjust to fit the challenge.

And yes, thinkers feel and feelers think. Everyone does both. It's all a matter of degrees.

Do people change? Yes. Do they flip from T to F and back again? Sometimes. It depends. Most of us stay pretty consistent in our temperament. If you exhibit only a slight preference for T over F or vice versa, it would not be extraordinary for you to sway back and forth daily.

Communication: Conflicts or Connections?

What is managing all about? When polled, Ts and Fs reveal quite different perceptions. Here's a beauty of an excerpt from a hard core T.

> All managing is about conflict—conflict with yourself, conflict with others, conflict with processes and procedures, conflict with data and projections, and so on. But mainly you hate managing because your performance, success, and job satisfaction is dependent on others. You can be a friggin' genius, and if you were an engineer, you'd be the talk of the company. But if you're a genius who happens to be a lousy manager, you're just a lousy manager. You hate managing because you have to depend on others and others have to depend on you and all of the complexities inherent to such a situation drive you nuts.

I could survive a week on that quote alone . . . I am easily amused.

And how did an F respond to the same question, What is managing all about?

> When you get down to it, managing is about creating connections and establishing a safe, respectful environment of open sharing and communication. Managing is connecting. The hardest part while supervising is to having to put my empathetic feelings aside and focus on behaviors. The part I hate is dealing with negative issues when an employee is not doing his job well.

What is so T and then so F about these two responses? Let's take a closer look.

The T uses the word *conflict* with ease, while the same word is laden with negativity and strife for an F. The T writes with customary authority, throwing around practical, objective measurements of professional success. He also doesn't mince words: There is no sugarcoating of opinions.

The F is almost apologetic for his opinion (both examples are from men). Mr. F uses "feeling" words—*create, safe, respectful, feelings.* The T speaks with objectivity—*process, procedure, data, performance, complexities.*

Glance through these responses again, noticing the cues tossed at us with the carefree ease and bounty of rice at a wedding. Don't worry; I won't force you to backtrack, losing ground in your success rate of pages clocked in the book. Reprinted and bolded here for your careful inspection.

THINKER RESPONSE DECODED

All managing is about **conflict**—**conflict** with yourself, **conflict** with others, **conflict** with **processes** and **procedures**, **conflict** with **data** and **projections**, etc. But mainly you hate managing because your **performance**, success, and job **satisfaction** is dependent on others. You can be a friggin' genius, and if you were an engineer, you'd be the talk of the company. But if you're a genius who happens to be a **lousy** manager, you're just a **lousy** manager. You hate managing because you have to depend on others and others have to depend on you and all of the **complexities** inherent to such a situation drive you nuts.

FEELER RESPONSE DEMYSTIFIED

When you get down to it, managing is about **creating connections** and establishing a **safe**, **respectful** environment of **open sharing** and communication. Managing is **connecting**. The hardest part while supervising is to have to put my **empathetic feelings** aside and focus on behaviors. The part I **hate** is dealing with **negative** issues when an employee is not doing his job well.

Once you get used to spotting telltale signs, it's a sport. Not an acceptable substitute for good old-fashioned cardio, though.

Comparisons for Your Consideration

Thinkers	Feelers
Lead with their heads	Lead with their hearts
Value and pursue logic	Value and pursue harmony
Crave fairness	Crave praise
Notice ideas more than feelings	Notice feelings more than ideas
Tend to be firm and tough	Tend to be caring and empathetic
Analyze	Interpret
May hurt others' feelings without knowing	May overpersonalize events
Can reprimand and not get emotional	Struggle with giving negative feedback
Potentially dissassociate from the impact of their action	Potentially over-identify with the feelings of the staff

That last item on the list reminds me of a high-ranking T in commercial real estate. He manages a demanding portfolio in a high-pressure environment. He sets collective goals, supports his staff, and is committed to his department. Consequently, he has a loyal, hard-working staff. He coined his own word: *wantitude*. He defines it as a merger of attitude and passion and says it's what he demands of himself and everyone around him. I asked him how he handles giving negative feedback. He smiled amicably, shrugged, and explained, "It's not hard for me to have those conversations. I'm not the one underperforming." His authentic style makes his T style of management work just fine.

Certain fields attract a higher-than-average ratio of Ts or Fs. For example, many nonprofits I work with have an abundance of Fs, whereas the financial industry often attracts a high percentage of Ts. Within organizations, the accounting department is likely to be heavily T and human resources primarily F.

At the same time, you might be surprised to discover a T surrounded by Fs in an earnest grassroots association or an F among Ts working in construction. When someone has a passion for her work, she can flex her style in any industry.

Likewise, Ts and Fs can pursue identical careers for divergent reasons. For example, we might assume high school English teachers are Fs who want to create a nurturing, warm environment full of positive reinforcement. However, I worked with a T high school English teacher. He taught the students structure and organization while preparing them with strategies for future challenges. Students said he was tougher on them than any previous teacher. He won teaching awards from his students year after year.

Full Disclosure. Well, Partial.

I'll come clean. I'm a . . . how to put this? Blazing feeler. Believe you me, it is not an easy way to live! Everything swirls round in feelers' heads endlessly as we psychoanalyze what was said to us, what we did or didn't reply, and how we feel about it.

However, I take it as a marvelous compliment that I am often mistaken for a thinker on the job. This doesn't mean thinkers are superior. If I was a strong thinker and the reverse happened I would feel equally pleased. Um, I mean, I would think it was evidence of my strength. The upshot is that managers of either temperament can learn to effectively flex their style so as to be indiscernible from the real deal.

Being flexible in how you communicate does not change your core. It does not mean being phony. Quite the opposite. Being a flexible manager requires strong self-knowledge, astute observation skills, and application of your innate strengths.

So I am a feeler who can kick into thinker mode as needed. This is only partial disclosure, because I also happen to be an introvert (see Chapter 9). So, in the end, I won't disclose a whole heck of a lot.

You've got to take what you can get.

CHAPTER THREE

Feelers Think and Thinkers Feel

He is happy whose circumstances suit his temper,

but he is more excellent who can suit his temper to any circumstance.

—David Hume

There once was a thinker named Fred

He managed by using his head

Until a feeler named Dawn

Said she felt like a pawn

So he flexed in the way that he led.

Chapter Highlights
- Distinguish thinker–feeler characteristics
- Explore related gender issues

I want to share with you a widely adapted parable of three blind men and an elephant, originating in ancient India. If you already know it, feel free to chime in. It goes something like this.

There are three blind men, each touching the same elephant—one at the tusk, one at a leg, one at the tail.

Each then describes the elephant by generalizing from the area he is feeling. They are in complete disagreement. The man feeling the tusk says an elephant is like a smooth pipe, the man at the leg says an elephant is like a pillar, and the man at the tail describes an elephant as being like a rope.

The three blind men approach the king to resolve their conflict. The wise king responds by saying they are all correct. He explains that an elephant has all the features described; they merely had different interpretations based on their vantage points.

The king maintained that people with a variety of perspectives can live harmoniously and truth can be described in different ways.

Keep this metaphor in mind as we proceed.

Feel-lings . . .
Nothing More than Feelings!

A BRIEF, *SENSITIVE* HISTORY OF FEELERS

Three things in human life are important. The first is to be kind. The second is to be kind. And the third is to be kind.

—Henry James

Just had to title this section with the Feeler National Anthem, alternative submissions welcome. You looking for something to appreciate today? Be glad this isn't an audiobook; I've been arrested for singing (among other things best left forgotten).

To shed some light on the F mind, I've put together a composite Q & A based on conversations with Fs at the workplace. The thinker section begins with a sample of T's distinctly divergent responses.

Q: Who bugs you?
A: Mean people.

Q: What do you want to say to them?
A: Why are you so mean? Would it kill you to be nice? How would you like to be treated that way?

Q: Really! Would you actually ask those questions?
A: No. It might hurt their feelings. Plus, I really don't want to get in an argument.

Q: What motivates you as a manager?
A: Making people who work with me fulfilled and happy in a caring environment where everyone is respected. I like making meaningful connections with my team.

Q: How can you flex your style to increase cross-temperament effectiveness?
A: I can TRY to not take things personally that supposedly have nothing to do with me . . . or to at least pretend I'm not upset.

Cut. That's plenty of data to get us started.

Feelers, I have a word of wisdom. It is a tough nut to swallow. Accept—even if you don't understand or like—this fact of life:

A whole bunch of people do not focus—at all—on feelings!

Feelings are not numero uno for everyone. Incredible, I know. Thinkers go about their business . . . well, going about their business. Allow yourself a moment of envy; it's okay. Can you imagine how freeing that would be? Now let it go; you are who you are.

And so are they.

They. Are. Not. Jerks.

They are practical, pragmatic, logical doers. They are darn handy to have around, believe you me. The more the merrier. As an aside, thinkers are generally extremely useful in a crisis. Learn to value and get along with thinkers.

Listen to what I am telling you here—I'll say it one more time for emphasis: Not everyone cares about feelings. This is a concept so foreign to off-the-chart feelers that it is nearly impossible to comprehend. So don't bother really trying to get it. Do yourself a favor and just believe it's true.

Now that we're on the same train, what are you going to do about it?

Don't bother answering; I will for you. You are going to carry a Q-tip everywhere you go.

What?

You heard me correctly. Go get a Q-tip. No, get a whole handful of them. Put one in your briefcase, one in your top left desk drawer, one in your pocket (take it out before washing), one in your car. You take it from there.

Perhaps you've never been let in on this well-kept (until now) secret. Q-tip is an acronym created exclusively for feelers.

Quit Taking It Personally!

That sounds a bit harsh at first. Judgmental, even. Put that luggage aside and be brutally honest with yourself. Let's make it real. You do take an awful lot personally. Remember the time that managing director didn't look at you in the elevator, the same one you thought you'd bonded with at the quarterly meeting? What about when the CEO avoided eye contact with you at the holiday party? Or the time four people in your department went out to lunch and you weren't invited? How about when the entire team you supervise celebrated completing the big project last year and no one thought you might like to join in? That was over a year ago!

Think of how much easier work would be if you took a lot fewer things to heart.

Want to hear something funny? When I bestow Q-tips on my F clients, they nearly always thank me warmly upon receiving this diminutive gift, even before they know why it is being given. The appreciation Fs have for the little things in life counterbalances their sensitivity on the other side. When meaning is piled on top of an otherwise run-of-the-mill Q-tip, I've caught Fs carrying it everywhere or prominently propping it on their desk. If Fs love anything, they love Meaning.

Fs' brains are whirling constantly, always processing the world around them. This trait makes them sensitive, perceptive, and often complex people.

And with that . . .

A Fact's a Fact

A BRIEF, PRACTICAL HISTORY OF THINKERS

I think, therefore I am.

     —René Descartes

Thinkers lead with their heads.

Hey, all you thinkers out there, raise your hand if you bothered to read the section on feelers rather than breezing past it to get to *your* segment. One . . . two-o-o . . .

I need to have a word with you. While I appreciate your honesty, I will now proceed to convince you it is in your own best interest to learn as much as you can about the feeler species and habitat.

How persuasive is the following? Grade my efforts:

> **It is important to care about your staff, to show them you really like them as people. You'll also feel better about yourself by demonstrating your warmth toward others.**

I hope you gave me a failing grade.

I wrote that just for kicks. I wanted to fail at convincing you. That's what a writer does for laughs to break up the *tap-tap-tap* on the keyboard. And half those taps are the backspace key.

Although the appeal above may work for a feeler, it nauseates a thinker. Or at least leaves you cold. Ahead is my second effort to convince you to read the feeler section.

Take two.

> **Educating yourself about feelers and what motivates them will increase their productivity. Also, you will become a more efficient manager while expending fewer resources.**

Better? Convinced? Now I hope you understand why it's worth-while for nonfeelers to read the segment "Feel-lings . . . Nothing More than Feelings." That title, by the way, is an exaggeration. Feelers *are* more than feelings. Okay, now scram. Then come directly back here when you've finished your catch-up assignment.

Now that you've at least skimmed the feeler section, you may be wondering why I didn't persuade the feelers to read this segment. They know the answer: Because they are already reading it.

It's time for our composite Q & A based on conversations with Ts on the job. Same questions as for the Fs, quite different responses.

Q: *Who bugs you?*
A: People who bring their feelings to the workplace.

Q: *What do you want to say to them?*
A: Grow up! We're all adults here. Leave your emotions at the door; we have a job to do.

Q: *Really! Would you actually say that?*
A: I would, except they'd make such a big deal out of it. It probably wouldn't be worth the effort.

Q: *What motivates you as a manager?*
A: Excelling. Pushing my staff beyond previous limits. Being fair and forthright.

Q: *How can you flex your style to increase cross-temperament effectiveness?*
A: I could probably thank people more, if I remember. It's really not my thing to go around complimenting people. It seems phony. I mean, we get paid to do our jobs.

Accept—even if you don't understand or like—this fact of life:

A huge herd of people cannot turn off their emotions at will!

I understand this is extremely alarming. It does no good to dispute or be annoyed by this fact. It won't ever go away! You're a smart cookie. You know better than to pound your fist on the desk—at least, for longer than a few minutes.

You are left with a single rational (gotcha with that word!) option: Work with it. No one is going to change to accommodate your will. You know that. You want to manage as efficiently as possible with maximum positive return on the investment of your time, energy, and resources.

Take this advice: Learn how to deliver timely, specific, sincere positive feedback to your direct reports. Put it on your to do list until it comes naturally. Demonstrating appreciation is a fast, free way to improve morale and productivity. Plus, it takes virtually zero time.

You'll thank me later. Or whatever; save it for your team.

It's easy to be lured into the urban legend that feelers don't think. Nothing could be further from the truth, I assure you. They are thinking all the time. Constantly. Hardly a moment passes that feelers aren't thinking.

(Mostly about their feelings, but never mind that.)

Another temptation is the reckless assumption that Fs are incapable of making tough decisions, or at the very least, good decisions. That's a popular T bandwagon, and it's oh so enticing to hop aboard. Resist!

There is zilch evidence that Ts make better decisions than Fs. Each species just goes about the deciding of stuff *really* differently. Ts base important decisions primarily on facts. Fs make big decisions based on . . . you guessed it . . . their feelings!

This may irk you. Yet, take hiring as an example. Tracking retention rates across industries, there's no discernible difference in success between managers who hire primarily based on "a good feeling" and those who select candidates based on objective criteria.

Now that we've highlighted the big ol' differences between Ts and Fs, let's see what happens when we toss gender into the mix.

 ## Men, Women, and Stereotypes

By now you could be thinking, "Hmm . . . I wonder if there is a gender bias in all this." Don't feelers sound suspiciously like clichéd women and thinkers like stereotypical men?

Yes. And no.

The Myers–Briggs Type Indicator (MBTI)manual breaks it down like this:

- General overall population ⟶ 40 percent thinkers, 60 percent feelers
- General female population ⟶ 24.5 percent thinkers, 75.5 percent feelers
- General male population ⟶ 56.5 percent thinkers, 43.5 percent feelers[2]

As an MBTI certified practitioner for nearly twenty years, I'm more or less obsessed with Myers–Briggs. I follow the ebb and flow of population trends with the rapt attention of my son watching stats during the draft of his fantasy basketball league.

It's an exciting life, what can I say?

When I was studying for my first MBTI certification, the numbers were about 50/50 overall, with 65 percent of men testing as thinkers and 35 percent as feelers. Reverse it for women: 35 percent were thinkers and 65 percent were feelers. Somewhere along the way, and for a number of years, the statisticians told us there was no gender bias in T/F, that men and women were equally likely to be thinkers or feelers. This seemed a bit surprising to me; however, I went along with it, being the cooperative person I am. Yet current statistics swing in the other direction altogether! This is breaking news. Jump up and down, or at least swirl your arm in a couple circles, would ya?

Let's take these stats at face value. The way things land now; three-quarters of women are primarily feelers (keep in mind significant variation between mild, moderate, and strong preferences). Just a bit more than half of men are thinkers—meaning, of course, that just a bit less than half are feelers.

Feelers are taking over the world!

I'm as surprised as the next person. If this doesn't count as headline news, I don't know what does. I understand this is a highly disturbing tidbit of information to the thinkers of the world. I feel your pain. I mean, I think you will make it through. I know you will. Just don't take it out on the feelers, okay? It's not their fault, even though it is tempting to blame them. Especially since most Fs will apologize regardless.

Despite general populace statistics, every workplace is self-selecting and therefore apt to vary from standard percentages. For example, the Department of Justice is likely to have a higher percentage of male *and* female thinkers, and an animal shelter will have a disproportionally large percentage of feelers from both genders.

Where do problems arise for managers in the T/F stats? As you already deduced, stereotypes dictate that feelers encompass female characteristics, and thinkers sound suspiciously like a typical male prototype.

These associations are supported to a degree by the statistics—more women are feelers and more men are thinkers. That does not discount the fact that plenty of dominantly thinker women and dominantly feeler men exist, all over the place. Because the idea of a feeler male or a thinker female flies in the face of expectations, these folks face extra challenges as managers.

What can you do about this, you maverick female Ts and male Fs? It helps to have an awareness that your style is not typical for your gender, that it can cause some people to misunderstand or unfairly judge you. It's best to not let this aggravate you. Know it may happen, and let it go. That said, female Ts can heed feedback about "taking the edge off" in certain situations and male Fs can practice taking a well-researched, strong stance on important matters. Find a comfortable balance while remaining true to who you are.

If I am trying to regularly say about my strengths, as what does that about gender identity, male-domina attitudes about gender identity, really so insecure as and authenticity? Am I need to act like a a woman in an authoritative position, why ated profession that I think I need to see success? stereotype of a man in order to see success? haven't I appreciated the value of being a feeler.

Jumpin' Thru Hoops

She & He

The typical expectation is that women are feelers and men are thinkers. The statistical majority in both genders reinforces these assumptions. The result is an undercurrent of largely unconscious, unintentional prejudice against male feelers and female thinkers.

A. When most people meet a manager who happens to be male with strong thinker traits, what kinds of words do you suppose they use to describe his leadership style?

1.

2.

3.

B. When people meet a female manager with strong feeler traits, what words might be used to describe her?

1.

2.

3.

C. Now let's flip it. How might one describe the management style of a man who happens to be a strong feeler?

1.

2.

3.

D. And what about that female manager who exhibits strong thinker traits? How does she get pigeonholed?

1.

2.

3.

I have conducted this activity with countless managers. Typical descriptors for A are *strong* or *decisive*. For B, *kind* or *caring*. For C, *weak* or *incapable*. For D, *cold* or *insensitive*.

The very characteristics lauded in male thinker managers, such as being tough and firm, are frequently judged as negative traits in women. Conversely, when male feeler managers exhibit traits appreciated in female feelers, the men are often criticized for being too "soft."

As managers, we can hold ourselves responsible for noticing and reversing stereotypes as they occur in ourselves and in others.

CHAPTER FOUR

But I Liked My *Real* Job!

What you manage in business is people.
—Harold Geneen

I did not sign up for this
Not in my plan, not on my list
Never wanted to be in charge of you
And now my work is never through . . .

Unless you select the route of pure neglect, the demands of managing can make your head spin. A heap of tasks follows you around like a storm cloud in spring, making even your most Herculean efforts seem to fall short. You may *never catch up.* Drowning in paper, people, processes.

Ts, I understand what you're thinking. Fs, I feel your pain.

Even if managing wasn't on your radar when launching a career, you really can learn to accept and even enjoy the part of job called "being a manager."

 &*%$@# Overwhelmed

I hear you . . . and I appreciate your directness. Let's dish.

Anne Lamott wrote the bestseller *Bird by Bird: Some Instructions on Writing and Life.* Embedded in the title is a universal lesson that Anne explains in her book. She tells it like this:

> Thirty years ago my older brother, who was ten years old at the time, was trying to get a report on birds written that he'd had three months to write, which was due the next day. We were out at our family cabin in Bolinas, and he was at the kitchen table close to tears, surrounded by binder paper and pencils and unopened books on birds, immobilized by the hugeness of the task ahead. Then my father sat down beside him, put his arm around my brother's shoulder, and said, "Bird by bird, buddy. Just take it bird by bird."[3]

Ever since I first read *Bird by Bird,* years ago, this advice has pulled me through difficult times. When you are overwhelmed with all your duties, remember Anne's dad's advice. Bird by bird.

Thanks, Anne . . . and hats off to your procrastinating brother and smart dad.

Ch-Ch-Ch-Ch-Changes

There's another reason promotion to manager—or to a more senior level of management—is tough. It's because change of any kind is difficult. Even so-called positive change. Presumably we are supposed to be happy about "good" change. So we feel guilty, on top of everything else, for having a negative reaction to positive change.

Change, by definition, means a departure from the status quo. Positive change—a promotion, a partnership, a bigger sales territory, a new home—still signifies a loss, letting go of the familiar. What we know and are comfortable with is gone. A wise entrepreneur I know describes times of successful transition as "being positively challenged."

So cut yourself some slack. Part of the reason you miss your "real" (aka previous) job is because it was what you knew. Now you're playing by new rules, with new expectations and new demands. Easier on paper than in practice. It's okay, though. Believe it or not, you'll get the hang of it.

I Gotta Be Me!

Here's a floatie to grab hold of when swirling into the riptide of managing. The only person you can be really well is yourself. Recall the Royal Rule presented in chapter 2: Be you.

Many of us forget this minor detail.

Remembering that you are, first and foremost, *yourself* is the first step toward being a successful (T!), happy (F!) manager.

**The only way you can aspire to managerial
greatness is by channeling yourself.**

As a senior executive in the tech industry wisely advised, "Don't try to be someone you're not. Managers come in all shapes and sizes, and the more you stay true to who you are, the harder people will work for you."

Here's the corollary to being yourself. Ready for this heady piece of reality?

You are not anyone else.

Take a moment to let this reality-altering whopper sink in. The ramifications are mind-boggling. You no longer need to decide for anyone else what they think or feel, the motivation behind other people's behavior, the rightness or wrongness of their decisions, the validity of their actions, or the justification for their inactions.

What a relief! Wipes clean a major chunk of the items to analyze in your overburdened managerial mind. What are you going to do with all your spare time?

I've just the thing to fill it. As it turns out, there are three rather pressing items over which you have complete and utter control . . . and responsibility. In fact, these are the only items you control. You might want to write them down.

**Your sole areas of direct responsibility are
your thoughts, your words, and your actions.**

Narrows things down, doesn't it? Ponder this. Go ahead; think of a single additional item over which you have direct control. Nada.

Getting down to it, you really need to direct your attention to the person behind the curtain. The one moving all those gears and pulleys, with the handy smoke and mirrors available on an as-needed basis. That would be you. It is tempting (and easy) to direct attention outside ourselves. Doing so lets you off the hook and results in a whole lot of nothing. As the owner of a financial services firm quipped, "Just give up on the idea you can control others."

Although don't managers have to, well, *manage* other people? Isn't that what this is all about? Let's recall from chapter 1 our handy-dandy definition of managing:

**Managing is the high-wire act of balancing
useful guidance and getting out of the way.**

Getting out of the way, once we get the hang of it, is easy. It means stepping aside and letting others do what they're there to do, rather than suffocating them with our interference and brilliant plans. Useful guidance is providing structure, sharing expectations, and being available to contribute to others' success.

None of that involves efforts to control anyone else's attitude, approach, or personality. We are too busy monitoring and consciously choosing our own thoughts, words, and actions to waste our time doing the impossible—being in charge of other people's inner worlds. Yet, by using our words and actions well, we can *influence* the responses and behaviors of others. As an executive vice president of a public relations firm put it, "The only way to get people to do what you want is to get them to want to do it. I have to give you something you want, like appreciation, recognition, importance."

Useful guidance, get out
of the way!

Testing and Revising Beliefs

This skill can entirely change your viewpoint and subsequent relationships. Think of beliefs you hold to be true about others. Next, rewrite the sentence, inverting the subject and object, as demonstrated in the following chart. Practice saying the revised sentence aloud and ask yourself about the likelihood that the new sentence is likely to be as true or truer than the original sentence. Try these on for size:

My Current Belief	Reversing the Subject to Challenge My Belief
He does not consider my feelings.	I do not consider his feelings.
You do not show interest in my projects.	I do not show interest in your projects. (or) I do not show interest in my projects.
She did not notice my nonverbal cues.	I did not notice her nonverbal cues.
He does not take my concerns into account.	I do not take his interests into account.
She argues with me.	I argue with her.
Others don't pay attention to my needs.	I don't pay attention to others' needs. (or) I don't pay attention to my needs.

Believing we know what is in someone else's mind presupposes supernatural powers. Presumably you know what other people think! That means you're a mind reader, with knowledge of others' inner thoughts. If that's the case, you really owe it to your country to work for their intelligence agency.

Otherwise, it's worthwhile to acknowledge that the rest of us never really know what is in someone else's head.

**Nearly always, when we attribute a belief or opinion
to someone else it means we have it ourselves.**

Take My Job, Please!

What if you really, really do yearn for your previous, nonmanagerial position?

Fredrico was a 35-year-old attorney working for a large U.S. agency. Within a year of receiving a promotion to a management position, he demoted himself.

You read that correctly; put the reading glasses away.

Why would a young professional in the midst of building a career and a personal life go so far as to reverse a promotion? You get one guess. Think context.

In Fredrico's promoted role he got to manage a herd of other attorneys in addition to handling his own, scaled-back legal work. Fight the urge to spout off a slew of lawyer jokes (though if you have a good one, send it to me).

Fredrico's decision didn't have to do with attorneys but with managing. He preferred to stall—perhaps arrest—his career trajectory to relieve himself of management responsibilities. He decided he would be happier, more fulfilled, and less stressed if he went back to being responsible only for himself.

Several years later Fredrico remained pleased with his choice. He enjoyed more autonomy, more flexibility, and shorter hours than his peers who took and kept comparable promotions.

Self-demotion is not an unheard-of phenomenon. The key is to be clear about your aspirations and goals. Fredrico's choice ended up being wise for him, if unconventional. Upon accepting a managerial position, you are making a decision to assume significant additional responsibilities and challenges.

There is nothing wrong with committing to a purely technical, nonmanagement career. As one CEO in sales and business development put it, "If you don't believe you can handle the added responsibility of being a manager—or just don't want to—don't take the job. I have seen great salespeople promoted to managers only to see them fail. I have also seen the opposite to be true. Sometimes, however, you are great at sales and should stay there."

In the case of Fredrico, choosing to decline a promotion to management required the certitude and courage to be true to himself.

Let's say you don't want to self-demote, yet hope on some less-than-rational level that you can hold a management position without having to actually, you know, manage. Maybe being a solid team player is good enough, you'll only manage self-starters, or you'll just assume the less-is-more management style.

I've got news for you: Management is not an aberration that interferes with your job. Take that belief, write it down, crumple it up, and toss it into the garbage (or, uh, recycling) bin in your workspace. Now do the responsible thing and get up, pick it up off the floor where it actually landed, and place it in the bin.

Hello, logotherapy. Everything tastes better with meaning.

Logotherapy

Victor Frankl, psychotherapist, developed logotherapy as the culmination of his personal and professional experience. Logotherapy is founded on the premise that meaning makes life purposeful. Frankl maintained that responsibility and meaning are linked. He explains in his book *Man's Search for Meaning* that the search to find meaning in one's life is a human being's primary motivational force.

Meaning can come from any number of sources and is both specific and unique. Regardless of how you define meaning, it is darn important. Frankl cites a Johns Hopkins University study on this topic. Researchers surveyed eight thousand students at forty-eight colleges as part of a two-year study sponsored by the National Institute of Mental Health. When asked what they considered "very important," only 16 percent gave highest marks to "Making a lot of money," whereas 78 percent listed as their primary goal "Finding purpose and meaning in my life."[4]

Money does not, apparently, buy meaning—or happiness.

According to Frankl, *independent of circumstance,* one can choose a life of despair, anger, hopelessness, and hostility or a life rich with meaning and purpose springing from a larger sense of purpose. Frankl's firsthand experience surviving in concentration camps enabled him to witness and experience, in the lowest imaginable human circumstance, that choices can be correlated with survival itself. He explained that in concentration camps all circumstances conspire to make prisoners lose hold of meaning. All familiar goals are taken away. Frankl called what remained "the last of human freedoms": the ability to choose one's attitude in a given set of circumstances.

Frankl observed average people, thrown into inexplicably inhuman situations, who proved to have a capacity to transcend despicable circumstance and discover guiding truths. Rising above an outward hell, some prisoners were able to lift themselves out of despair by creating purpose through assisting others.

On a more accessible level, identifying a unique purpose and contribution on the job can give you and those around you, the lift you need to thrive. The greater your responsibility (as you ascend the management ranks), the greater your potential for meaning.

There is a correlation between excelling and investing one's work with meaning. Those who go above and beyond in their work also report the highest levels of workplace satisfaction. The more energy invested, the greater the exhilaration of putting skills to maximum use.

Apply beginner's mind even if you are a manager!

On a Related Note

☆ The Impostor Phenomenon ☆

Many managers harbor a secret, doomed sense of being fraudulent—if others only knew how incompetent and over their heads they really are!

The mid-1980s yielded a gem of a book entitled *The Impostor Phenomenon*,[5] which attracted a much-deserved cult following. The gist is that what many of us present externally is worlds apart from how we feel inside.

The book opens with a vignette of a successful businessperson working a room. Step inside the same person's mind, however, and an entirely different interpretation of reality is revealed.

The book's platform is that many seemingly successful leaders secretly believe themselves to be impostors and that if the rest of us realized what ill-equipped fakers they really are, their entire facade would crumble apart.

This phenomenon is alive and kickin' in the twenty-first century. Plenty of marvelously qualified people view themselves as alarmingly inept at navigating the business worlds in which they find themselves. The higher they rise, the greater the sneaking suspicion that this has all been a big mistake, that they somehow lucked into this leadership role.

Amplifying this belief is the fact that the higher one climbs the corporate ladder, the less likely senior executives are to pursue professional development opportunities.

I see this link reflected in my leadership development seminars. When I facilitate a program for a crowd of up-and-comers, they typically soak in knowledge like luminous sponges on the Great Barrier Reef.

Seasoned pros, on the other hand? Except for a rare breed, most attend professional development opportunities only under duress, convinced they already know it all.

Becoming a general counsel, partner, C-suite resident, or achieving some other form of "success" means you have achieved technical success in your field. It does not necessarily correlate with being a talented, knowledgeable, or inspirational leader. Being a lifelong learner is a practical way to combat the perception that you are an imposter. Not to mention improving your management skills. There, I mentioned it.

Prove It

What is the best guarantee you won't be considered fraudulent? That your true intentions will be believed? A few years back, I found the following Lewis Cass quote taped to the front of a client's door:

> **People may doubt what you say, but they will believe what you do.**

Rambling on about your commitment to the team won't convince anyone you care. Chipping in to help with a project because you want them to shine? You don't need to say a word and they know where you stand.

Sample Example

Trashy Leadership

Monica had been preparing a presentation for weeks. Two days before the event, she put the finishing touches on a poster-sized storyboard.

And then...! The night before the big conference Monica couldn't find her storyboard anywhere. It seemed to have vanished into the fourth dimension. Slowly the realization hit her that the maintenance crew might have tossed out her carefully crafted presentation, mistaking it for garbage. Nearing panic, she poured out her suspicions to Drew, her supervisor. He excused himself from the room.

Monica didn't know where he had disappeared to until she glanced out a window overlooking the back of the building. There was Drew in the Dumpster, sleeves rolled up, searching for Monica's presentation poster. She called over her colleagues, who were also working late to prepare for the next day.

Drew found it. He thought what he did was no big deal. He expected 100 percent from his department and always gave at least that much himself. He loved his job and was known to be authentic in all his dealings. He led quietly, with no observable ego interference.

Drew returned upstairs to a team that would run a hundred miles for him in the rain.

Expanding Your Reach

Self-aware human beings make the best managers. Skeptical? Isn't putting together a solid structure and smart team enough? No. Don't believe me? Let's flip it. Recall a terrible manager you've come across in your trials and travails traversing the globe. My wild guess is he had the self-awareness of a barnacle.

So the first step is looking in the mirror, knowing who you are. That's not quite enough, however. Ready for part two?

For the second step, we put the mirror aside. Don't worry; your hair looks fine.

Fortified with strong self-knowledge, you are now ready to leverage your strengths to meet other people where they are. I call this *flexing*, an exceptionally valuable, versatile management skill. Don't expect others to speak your language, understand your motives, or change to suit your whims. Most people just aren't that skilled. It is up to you.

Being flexible in how you relate to and motivate others does not mean compromising fairness. Within the context of holding everyone to the same standards of performance and conduct, you can adapt your language, feedback techniques, and modes of reinforcement.

Starting with chapter 5, a wrap-up "Flex" and a P.S. will conclude each chapter. Just like an *amuse-bouche,* except those start a meal and often fit on a spoon.

CHAPTER FIVE

Flex for Success

There is no mystery about successful business . . .
Exclusive attention to the person who is speaking to you.
—Charles Eliot

Meeting other peeps where they are at
Sure beats falling on your own face, splat
Gotta drop the ego, a fact's a fact
Flexing is the ticket, and that is that.

Life isn't neat and tidy. Neither, therefore, is managing. Sometimes we bang our heads against the wall; sometimes we need the visceral sting. Other times, we can face the facts calmly. We all carry baggage, harbor distinguishing quirks, and maintain astonishingly diverse responses to the world at large. These facts of life display no observable intention of ever going away, so we may as well learn how to understand and amicably appreciate the people we manage, near and far, formally and informally. As this occurs, our work as managers becomes much easier . . . even (gasp!) enjoyable.

How is such a tremendous feat accomplished? Do you need nerves of steel, superhuman patience, and the ability to leap buildings in a single bound? And don't you already have enough swirling around in your busy, busy brain? No sweat. Well, perhaps a few tiny droplets of perspiration, easily wiped away.

Your success—and fulfillment—as a manager is neatly encased in one bite-sized nugget:

Be who you are, just flex your style to manage others.

What a mysterious statement. Let's dissect, shall we?

Be who you are . . .

D'oh! Who else would you be? A fine question.

This book guides you to carve out a distinctive brand of management from your natural strengths. No one size fits all sold in this book.

. . . just flex your style to manage others.

What does this sweet little, unassuming phrase mean? Why must we follow its mandate? And how? Take a number and find a seat.

Flexing your style means being versatile in how you lead, communicate, and motivate. A tough approach propels one employee; mild-mannered encouragement inspires another. Being flexible requires proficiency in a range of techniques, to draw upon as needed.

This does not require disregarding your own temperament.

It means maximizing rapport with others
while maintaining your core of integrity.

Flexing your style does not mean holding people to varying standards—accountability remains consistent across the board. All that changes is how you manage and motivate different personality styles.

Implementing this high-level concept requires two challenging skills: the aptitude to assess others' temperaments and the ability to modify your communication style on the fly.

Plenty of us jump to conclusions on a regular basis. If only we could accumulate frequent flyer mileage, then we'd really be going places. Examples include jumping to the conclusion that others have the same perspective as we do or that only our opinion could possibly make sense.

Keep in mind that people are often speaking different languages, figuratively, even when the words sound strikingly similar.

What's a modern manager to do?

The best response is to Pay Attention. We are bombarded daily with a veritable tsunami of information about how people process the world and what motivates them. What do average-to-middling managers do with this valuable information? Breeze right on by, without so much as a backward glance. Like receiving a gift and tossing it right back at the giver. They are apparently far too busy, preoccupied, or

If you're reading this book beginning to end (so organized!) and have reasonable retention skills, you will recall an opening *Phantom Tollbooth* analogy. Here's another.

Milo, the young protagonist, his best pal Tock (a watch dog), and the Humbug (a large bug) are driving along on a beautiful day.

"Nothing can possibly go wrong now," cried the Humbug happily, and as soon as he'd said it he leaped from the car, as if stuck by a pin, and sailed all the way to [a] little island.

"And we'll have plenty of time," answered Tock, who hadn't noticed that the bug was missing—and he, too, suddenly leaped into the air and disappeared.

"It certainly couldn't be a nicer day," agreed Milo, who was too busy looking at the road to see that the others had gone. And in a split second he was gone also.

Turns out, they appeared on the Island of Conclusions. When they ask a local resident how they got there, he replies,

"You jumped, of course . . . That's the way most everyone gets here. It's really quite simple: every time you decide something without having a good reason, you jump to Conclusions whether you like it or not . . .

"Getting back is not so easy. That's why we're so terribly crowded here."
The trio eventually swims back through the Sea of Knowledge, at which point Milo declares, "[F]rom now on I'm going to have a very good reason before I make up my mind about anything. You can lose too much time jumping to Conclusions."[6]

Quite.

important to match their management style to the personalities on their team. The result? They are ineffective and frustrated.

That is *so* not you.

You know better than that. You focus on your team, noticing nuances about their language, their office decor, and preferred project assignments. You pay careful attention, calibrating your approach

Chilly Reception

For more than twelve years I was a regular at a local gym. It is safe to say I was well known, and although there was a policy to check all gym identifications upon entry, this formality had long since been waived for me.

One day a new guy showed up at the front desk. Turnover tended to be high, especially for the 5:00 to 10:00 a.m. shift, so this was a typical occurrence. However, within a couple of weeks life would revert to normal and my gym ID would be tucked back away, allowing easy, fast entrance, unencumbered by the time and formality of showing and scanning a card.

This new guy, however, relentlessly demanded to see my ID every day—in a monotone voice, to make matters worse. There was only one logical explanation: He was a jerk. I decided I hated him. Every morning I'd grit my teeth, slowing down my rushed routine for this wretched guy who clearly knew I was a member. This was a gym not an airport! How serious do we really need to be?

My mornings were being encumbered, and it was his fault!

Then, one day I had a revelation.

He was just doing his job. Maybe he was not a jerk. Maybe he was highly responsible. Maybe he took his straightforward job very seriously. Maybe he was the best front desk employee the gym had ever had.

The next day I showed up at my usual time, learned his name (James), and introduced myself. I told James I could tell he did a great job working the front desk, that they were lucky to have found him. And, with my reframing, I really meant it. Imagine the extra energy, commitment, and devotion it takes to check everyone's ID rather than just doze behind the desk and let people flow in.

We became friendly; he started greeting me by name. Along the way I realized James was shy, so he didn't initiate connections with the members streaming in each morning. Yet he welcomed a friendly face, which mine had become.

One day I was relaying this story to a coaching client and he asked the kicker question: When did James stop checking my ID?

James continued to check my ID; he never stopped. The difference was that I was now prepared for the ritual, offering my card up easily each morning as we greeted each other, inquiring about weekends, the weather, or recent events. Shifting one's perceptions and actions does not rely on expecting others to change. The only change required is in our own minds. We have control.

Reframing the scenario to determine that I caused the friction, not James, gave me the freedom to change the scenario without altering a single external factor—except his response to my radically different expectations and behavior. James went from rude to friendly. Or did I?

Looking back, I can see he was a T doing his job. I was an F looking for a friendly connection. Neither of us changed who we are; we just met midway at a comfortable working medium.

to match your observations about their style. You know that to flex your style effectively you've got to make educated guesses about what works for different people, making adjustments along the way.

I've got news for you, sunshine. What we're talking about here is a lifetime commitment. Like a mobile phone contract, only worse. Or like physical fitness—you can't exercise one week and cross health off your list of things to do. Flexing your style is a line item to work on throughout your tenure as a manager. That's okay; it grows on you after a while.

Flexing requires customizing your communication to motivate different staff members. If you are a flaming F, you need to behave as an off-the-chart T at times to accomplish your F mission statement. You can become so skilled at impersonating a T that an innocent bystander may confidently proclaim you to be a T. Yet you remain an F at your core, flexing your style, brilliantly.

What you see is not always what you get. This doesn't mean you are artificial. You have nothing in common with fruit roll-ups containing no actual fruit.

You needn't change your inherent personality to be a gifted and committed manager. You merely acquire the skill set of motivating different people in different ways. Gold stars, all around.

A word to the wise: Don't cool your heels waiting for others to meet you at your spot on the temperament continuum. Make that your job; save yourself the aggravation.

What You Say Is What You Get

There are endless clues about whether the people working for you are Fs or Ts.

Here's an example. You accompany two of your staff to a lunch-and-learn and they have very different reactions to the subject discussed.

On the way back to the office, they enter into an animated discussion about their divergent perspectives.

Does their disagreement seem to be

- a matter of little or no consequence, or

- a source of anxiety or stress?

A strong T will take a difference of opinion as a matter of little consequence; a strong F will feel stress from the same situation. A slight thinker or slight feeler will have mixed, milder reactions.

Think about why this is so. Or shall I say, why do you feel this is so? Time for class.

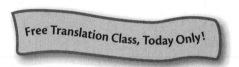

Free Translation Class, Today Only!

Welcome to your lucky day. You happened to turn to this page on the day we're offering free translation lessons! You're just in time. Take a seat; help yourself to some murky coffee with powdered creamer (now there's an oxymoron). We're about to get started.

By now you understand that thinkers and feelers have distinctive versions of reality and divergent decision-making tactics. It's no surprise they also speak different languages.

Don't walk out! Professor Zack here, at your service. Rosetta Stone is an admittedly more comprehensive—albeit more costly—program.

The following chart highlights examples of how to translate what one tribe says into the other's vocabulary.

Thinkers	Feelers
So, what do you think?	How do you feel about that?
I think this meeting will be worthwhile.	I have a good feeling about this meeting.
What did you think about that program?	How did you feel about that program?
I don't like dealing with pushovers.	I don't like dealing with rude people.
Conflict is a healthy part of any team.	We need to cooperate to avert conflict.

This is quite a hoot when you get the hang of it. Then again, perhaps you have a real life.

The first step is noticing when people use the words *think* and *feel*. These two words are generally interchangeable, as in the following example:

I **think** it's a good idea. —➤ I **feel** it's a good idea.

Both of these options can be restated with neutral words, nonspecific to Ts or Fs:

I **know** it's a good idea. —➤ I **believe** it's a good idea. —➤

I **sense** it's a good idea. —➤ It **seems** like a good idea.

Nonspecific words are good choices when you want to make neutral statements without a bias toward either group.

Here's a list for your use.

Appreciate	Experience	Perceive	Remember
Believe	Generate	Ponder	Seem
Comprehend	Know	Process	Sense
Decide	Learn	Realize	Support
Demonstrate	Motivate	Relate	Understand

For beginners, the first level is to listen for the frequency with which a staff member uses variations of the words *think* and *feel.* In conversation, these words are nearly always technically interchangeable.

Let's say you attend a training program at work and walk out of the classroom at lunchtime with your colleague, Aaron. You engage in casual conversation and, although nothing is wrong with the exchange, you sense a vague disconnect. This can occur when the conversation goes along these lines:

> You: Hey, Aaron. So what'd you think about the training class this morning?
> Aaron: Oh, hi! I felt good about it.

> You: Really? Do you think you learned anything?
> Aaron: Sure do! I feel like I picked up a lot of useful tips.

> You: Yeah, I guess you're right. I think I did, too. Took a while to get going.
> Aaron: Plus, I felt like introducing everyone at the start was worthwhile.

> You: You think so?
> Aaron: Definitely, because it felt good to finally learn names of the new people.

Notice what's happening? As you tune in to the use of these primary words (*think, thought,* versus *feel, felt*), you will be amazed at the consistency with which many people favor one over the other. This is a solid clue for those on either end of the T/F continuum.

The next step is to practice both languages so you become equally conversant in both, with the ability to speak in Thinker or Feeler at will. With practice, you can match language in important conversations. For example, in an annual performance review with a thinker, shift into thinker language to ensure your message is heard.

Sample words favored by Ts:

- Principles
- Fairness
- Analysis
- Consistency
- Validity
- Rationale

Sample words favored by Fs:

- Compassion
- Empathy
- Caring
- Sensitivity
- Intensity
- Harmony

What comes naturally, with no effort, to those at one end of the temperament spectrum can take much conscious effort for those at the other end. Although one workplace interaction may roll off a T's back, the same event may upset or confuse an F, and vice versa.

Here are some potential on-the-job danger zones:

Thinkers may

- lack awareness of the impact of their tone;
- make decisions solely based on logic;
- be unaware or unconcerned with interpersonal discord; or
- value what is "true" over what is subjectively best for the team.

Feelers may

- be particularly sensitive to conflict;
- make decisions based on relationships;
- react with strong feelings to interpersonal challenges; or
- value what is "good" over what is objectively best for the team.

If you are an auditory person, listening for the frequency of T and F language will be especially useful in identifying style preferences. Another way to identify thinkers and feelers is through visual clues.

Natural Habitat

A good place to collect visual cues about personality style is in the work environment. Begin by taking a peek at a few workspaces as you mosey down the hall.

The natural habitat of a feeler will usually have at least a few photographs, more likely many. It doesn't matter if they are old or recent, family or friends. Feelers are also likely to display certificates earned for one-day trainings or long-outdated events. Often a favorite quote is framed or just taped to the computer monitor for frequent reference.

Feelers
Free Advice for the Thinker Manager

Thinkers. Listen to me, would you? Take a few minutes—fifteen or twenty tops. It won't crush your productivity. If anything, it's a useful diversion. Hang a few diplomas, awards, and credentials up; they build credibility. Bring in some favorite, somewhat relevant books and stick 'em on your bookshelf so it's not all manuals. It builds ambiance without being touchy-feely.

And display at least one photo, even if it's your dog. Gives visitors something to look at when you invite them in for a meeting.

Although organization—or the lack thereof—is not directly linked to the Thinker–Feeler continuum, it is fair to say a feeler's office is more prone to clutter, merely due to the fact that he has more items of sentimental value filling the space. And nearly anything can be magically bestowed with sentiment by a feeler.

Thinkers' work environments are quite different. I have entered clients' offices that appear recently moved into. To be more specific, not yet moved into. Any intended wall hangings stand leaning against the wall. There are virtually no personal items whatsoever.

Welcome to the thinker's natural habitat. This lack of decoration can be so extreme that one is tempted to wonder whether this is a shared workspace or the thinker is here only temporarily while his real office is renovated. Go ahead and ask. No worries. The question won't hurt the thinker's feelings. I've fallen for this misconception several times. More often than not, the response will be along the lines of what I heard from a vice president in global development: "No, this is my office. [Laughs.] I moved to this site about eighteen months ago. I keep meaning to put stuff up, just haven't had the time. I'm not in here much anyway."

Don't be fooled. The supposed stuff won't be up for display on your next visit either.

Why such an activity? Because in addition to awareness and sensitivity to differences, building cohesion among coworkers is one of the best things you can do for your team. A recent study found significantly lower levels of stress in work environments where the employees reported strong, supportive relationships.[7]

Jumpin' Thru Hoops

Don't Panic!

Here's a quick activity to do with your team to prove that people have plenty in common—even thinkers and feelers.

This activity works with either newly formed or well-established teams of approximately five to fifteen people. Start by saying something along these lines: "Don't panic! However, I have some alarming news! You are a group of people with absolutely nothing in common!" Then write the following on a whiteboard or easel for all to see (or have it prepared in advance):

People with

Absolutely

Nothing

In

Common

Notice (and bring to the group's attention, if necessary) that this is an acrostic, with the first letter of each word forming the word *panic*.

You will then proceed to amaze the crowd, proving your highly scientific, well-researched point. Instruct everyone to write down a fact about themselves that they are reasonably certain is *not true about anyone else present*. Born in Anchorage, for instance (as long as you are not headquartered in Alaska). Youngest of seven siblings. Can juggle fire on a unicycle. That sort of thing.

Have participants take turns stating their unique facts. If someone else there does share the trait, the participant must drum up a new one. Easy.

Upon the conclusion of the activity, you will have learned unique facts about everyone on the team. At this point you can loudly draw everyone's attention to the fact that you are, once again, correct! They have absolutely nothing in common with each other.

Now is the time for your hairpin turn. Say, "Wait! Perhaps there is another angle to this. We must consider the missing link." Think Darwin, if you must.

Request a volunteer; let's call her Marci. Usher Marci front and center. Marci's job is to begin speaking without pause about her life—starting point anywhere. Everyone else listens carefully. The moment Marci says something that also rings true for another person present (attended University of Wisconsin! Love eighties music! Crazy for sushi!), that person calls out "Pause!," springs forward, and stands next to Marci up front. At this point, Marci ceases her verbal stream-of-consciousness autobiography and the next person starts talking about himself. That is, until someone else says "Pause" and picks up where he left off.

The result is a line of teammates, linked together by what they have in common. *Meraviglioso!*

(This is my favorite Italian word. Means "marvelous." Isn't it, just?)

Team-building activities to bolster camaraderie are not just something to fill time at a staff retreat. Encouraging teamwork and fostering affinity among employees correlates with lower workplace stress, higher morale, and improved productivity.

 Flex!

Flex your style to meet Ts and Fs where they are—don't expect others to have the communication acuity to meet you halfway.

P.S. Respect different models of the world.

CHAPTER SIX

Lonely @ the Top

Everybody likes a compliment.

—Abe Lincoln

You make me so lonely baby
I get so lonely
I get so lonely I could die.
(So I didn't write this one. Elvis, "Heartbreak Hotel")

Who wants to spend the day ordering people around . . . other than a bored older sister? Endless to do lists combined with a constant blast of pressures (not to mention those omnipresent meetings) can cause even a seasoned boss to snap. Yet you can learn how to balance pressures while simultaneously motivating others to excel.

It turns out that simple workplace friendships with direct reports aren't so simple after all. You went from being one of the gang to being one of one. Sure, you understand things are different when you're In Charge. You're still the same friendly, supportive person, though. Why are you on the outside?

How does it happen?

Back to the Beginning

A promotion opportunity presents itself—what you've been visualizing into fruition for three long years. You furtively hope they hire from within, not some no-name, no-good hotshot who knows nothing about your industry. You and several of your peers apply. Jackpot! A wise executive management team selects you. You dedicate a glorious Sunday to moving your files and tchotchkes out of your cube and into an office with a real door.

You decide, in a flash of brilliance, to welcome in the new era under your reign by greeting everyone on Monday morning with a sponsored-by-you bagel breakfast.

You arrive an hour early, humming to yourself, and set up the lunchroom with all the best finishing touches. You make a little sign imploring your newly acquired staff to Help Yourself!, courtesy of you. You tastefully retreat to your office so as not to hover, and await a flood of gratitude.

Manners are a thing of the past, you declare silently to yourself by 11 a.m. You punch the keyboard with more gusto than is strictly necessary to send off a flurry of e-mails explaining the new systems you've been dying to put in place. Not one person has thanked you for the bagel breakfast you provided, let alone congratulated you on your new title and digs.

What is up with that?

Everything changes now. Your cronies are now your employees, and the two don't mesh. You're reminded of when your mom helpfully noted, "I'm not your friend! I'm your mother!" As if there was any confusion about the matter.

I've got stinky news. Please sit down. Ta-ta to work relationships as you knew them. Now you're their boss, not their bud.

To be clear, all the others who vied for your position believe they deserved it more than you. They're mad. Plus, they will search for evidence to confirm their theories by waiting for you to mess something up, and it won't take long (I don't mind being the person to tell you). They knew you weren't qualified.

Which brings us to cognitive dissonance.

We just have be right, don't we? We do. In fact, there's an incredibly strong drive to be right. When we have a belief in the world and evidence disproves this belief, our brains go into overdrive to dispute that data. Sometimes we don't even *process* the evidence. Cognitive dissonance can cause people to negate information that contradicts preexisting belief systems.

Let's put together the pieces. The others who competed for your job believed they deserved it. This can easily lead to the idea that you intervened between them and their rightful promotion. So, at least initially, it'll be difficult for them to accept you as qualified for the position. You'll have to work to win them over. Not impossible, just lots of time, patience, and rapport building.

Also, sooner or later you're going to have to give everyone else who works for you performance feedback. That's generally no walk in the park. Particularly if an inadequate system precedes you and folks are used to coasting through, you have your work cut out for you. It's best to work on positive relationships early on in your tenure . . . while maintaining your authority, of course.

What if you have one really, *really* good friend at work—actually you consider him your best friend—and you're certain this relationship, at least, will remain intact through the storm of your promotion.

Perhaps you're right. For every rule, there is an exception. Still, not to be Ms. Doom 'n' Gloom, but this creates a whole new set of problems. You will—just expect it!—be accused of favoritism. You're both on the hot seat. People won't say this to your face. They will instead confirm each other's suspicions, with increasing agitation among the troops.

Every Step You Take

The higher you rise, the more you are analyzed, discussed, and observed.

For a select few, that's exciting. For most, it's a tough pill to swallow. Your every move in the presence of others is watched and interpreted. Did you ever realize how riveting you are?! Don't let it go to your head. A Thinker vice president of marketing with a creative edge and impatience for buy-in admitted, "I have gotten negative backlash—more than once, I'm sorry to say—when not aware enough of the impact of what I say or how I am saying it. Then I have to do damage control, which does not always work."

I don't envy the supremely famous. I figure that kind of life differs from imprisonment only in the backdrop. Imagine not being able to go to the park, playground, grocery shop, or neighborhood bistro without being scrutinized, photographed, and written up. Privacy vanishes as fast as a Top 20 pop song in the twenty-first century.

Assuming a leadership role within most professions invites nowhere near the level of scrutiny gracing superstars in sports, music, movies, and royal families, yet it certainly has a foothold on the continuum of being observed. Your selection of a venti triple-shot whip extra hot no foam skinny vanilla latte at the Starbucks in your company's lobby is unlikely to land you a front-page photo in the tabloids. It's just potential cause for a few of the masses behind you in the morning rush line to glance up from their iPhones, shooting you an irritated glare.

On the other hand, being in an influential position increases the ripple effect when you treat employees well, spearhead volunteer campaigns, and mentor new staff. The limelight brings potential for far-reaching impact as a positive role model.

Good with the bad, baby.

Let's talk about the impact of coaching styles. Our everyone-gets-a-trophy society is pretty gung ho about what I call feel-good behaviors. A manager's job is to make her staff feel good, right? Feel good about themselves, their tasks, and ultimately about her, too.

Imbalanced feel-good management backfires. A feel-good coach seeks opportunities to applaud efforts, believing this motivates people. Missing from the equation is a healthy mix of motivation and inspiration. A feel-good manager offers praise even for mediocre results.

Sample Example

Do Good or Feel Good?

My leadership programs frequently include activities that at first seem impossible to the participants. Teams are presented with a group challenge and are instructed to alert me when they believe they have done the best job possible given the resources they have.

More often than not, teams beckon me over quickly, asserting they have completed the task—at well below the level I know they can achieve. I do not accept their outcome and tell them I am certain they can do better. I remind them I am very busy and not to bother me again until results improve by 200 percent. Then I flounce away (the flounce is my favorite part).

Every team of the hundreds I have worked with exceeds its own expectations. Their enthusiasm is amusing, concluding with high fives, group photo ops, and embarrassing little dances.

What happened to dramatically improving outcomes . . . while also boosting morale?

In reality, inspiring people to *do* good prevails over the goal of making them merely *feel* good. Here's the clincher: Do-good leadership makes teams feel better than feel-good leadership.

The natural inclination of many feelers can initially sway them to be feel-good coaches. However, coaxing people to do better, to exceed their own expectations rather than halting at early efforts, ultimately makes both the coach *and* the team feel better. Excelling is a natural high. Plus the coach garners respect and admiration.

As a manager in a marketing company shared, "My boss is ultra-demanding, and though our styles are very different, she has influenced me to expect—and get—more from my employees as well."

When people do lackluster, run-of-the-mill work, they feel mediocre. In such cases, praise doesn't boost their sense of accomplishment; it merely diminishes the value of praise. They recognize that their

Jumpin' Thru Hoops

Coach Ticket

Take a pen and a moment. Close your eyes . . . while remaining conscious. Recall a favorite coach from any time in your life.

This can be a sports coach, supervisor, family member, teacher, mentor, friend—you get the general idea. The first person to enter your mind is generally the ticket.

My favorite coach: _____

Now create a list of adjectives that describe this person:

_____ _____ _____

_____ _____ _____

_____ _____ _____

_____ _____ _____

Reflect on your list. Was this a person a feel-good coach, a cheerleader? Or did this person push you further than you could have gone on your own—a do-good coach? In most cases, our best coaches are examples of tough love. We understand they are invested in us, believe in our potential, and are committed to our success. Their belief in us does not manifest in a sticky stream of superlatives. Rather, they razz and push and torment us to push, push, push through barriers. We strive hard to achieve their vision for our success.

To be an inspirational manager, demonstrate the characteristics you value, earn the respect of your team, and create a platform for them to jump higher than ever before.

manager has a low bar, so they do too. They feel average about the work product as well.

When pushed and challenged, we rise to the expectations to which we are held.

This hoop-jumping exercise proves the point. If you skipped over it, skip on back. It only takes a few moments and makes it personal. Push on through to the other side.

Consensus Is So Old-School

Involving your team in decision-making can seem like a big ol' Pandora's box, propelling many managers to go it alone. Yet a well-designed process builds ownership and dissipates the burden of solo decision-making.

Structure and perceived fairness are key. This next tool provides both. Presto!

I am anticonsensus. Even though usual workplace convention holds consensus on a pedestal. We need to reach consensus! Consensus required! Everyone must work toward consensus.

In typical work cultures, consensus can be a major energy, time, and resource drain. How the heck is it supposed to be reached, anyway? In any group larger than, say, two, consensus is a pretty lofty ambition. People have varying viewpoints, opinions, personalities, and perspectives. To say we aren't going to take action until we all agree is a bit nuts, yes? What happens when people don't agree? We sequester them in a boardroom for a few weeks and hope for the best?

What people really want is a sense of fairness. A belief that they are taken seriously and their points of view are honored. That is not the same thing as always "winning."

Enter multivoting. Multivoting has everything: simplicity, fairness, ease of use, flexibility, good looks.

Okay, maybe not that last one. Depends on the stickers used, I suppose. But I get ahead of myself.

Let's say you are in a group (six to one hundred people) who must either prioritize among a set of choices or make a decision about a direction to take.

Display the options in large print around the room, on easel paper or whiteboards. Provide each participant with three small stickers.

Anything will do—circles, stars, or go nuts and get artsy. I'm not so good at that stuff, myself.

Participants vote by putting the stickers under their selection(s). If a group member feels very strongly about a single, first choice, she will stick all three of her votes under the same option. If she has a first and second choice, she puts two stickers under number one and one under number two. If she has equal interest in three options, she can spread out all three stickers under different selections.

Rather than having group members just raise a hand for their first choice, multivoting enables them to demonstrate how strongly they feel about their choice . . . and to indicate what other option(s) they support to some degree.

Each time I use multivoting, a clear couple of winners emerge. The dots are concentrated in one to three top selections.

This technique is effective because no one feels dissed. It is a fair, open system. If I am only one of a few people voting for my top choice, I may feel disappointed, but I can't argue the fairness of the decision.

People are relieved to arrive at a decision in a fraction of the time taken up by tedious consensus building.

There are variations on multivoting to suit virtually any situation. You can make the voting process anonymous by having participants place stickers (or other markers) in envelopes rather than openly displaying them on a poster or whiteboard. It can be conducted virtually, online. It can be accomplished outside, with no walls or stickers, by having participants raise one, two, or three fingers and assigning an unbiased counter. You get the concept.

I have a deceptively simple activity in which I give teams of three to eight people a set of seven plastic geometric pieces, one in the shape of an arrowhead. Instructions are sparse: *Create five simultaneously existing arrowheads of the same size and shape, using the pieces provided.*

Piece of cake.

Some groups solve the challenge quickly, some take thirty minutes or more, some groups never solve the puzzle. Most groups realize it is easy to assemble four arrowheads and inform me there are not enough pieces for five. I carefully count the seven parts on their table and assure them that they have enough resources.

Have you ever worked with (or near) a team who made the same claim: "We don't have enough resources to achieve our task"? And then another, comparable team somehow accomplishes the impossible with the same or fewer resources?

Sometimes in this activity a participant will short circuit. He will cling to the notion that the challenge is impossible. Even as other teams around him triumphantly announce success, he will continue to pronounce this an unsolvable task doomed to failure. Over and over, he will repeat his conviction.

From experience, I know his team will fail. They always do. One vocal naysayer will smash any hope of success to smithereens. The most common mistake I see in these situations is the manager letting the negative voice go on too loud and too long before addressing or mitigating the situation. Negative energy can jeopardize the outcome of an entire team.

When you ignore or downplay the significance of a single person's negativity, the result spreads far beyond that individual. Speak to that person, look for the cause, discuss alternatives, ask for support. Don't let a small flame turn into a wildfire that destroys everyone's best efforts.

Parenthetically, the arrowhead puzzle requires thinking outside the box. Or, in this case, inside the arrowheads. Four arrowheads are created from the pieces provided and the fifth is created through the arrangement of the other four—in the negative space that appears when they are placed in the correct pattern. In case you were wondering.

Relationships: Bottom-Line Influence

Some executives believe results are what matter most, not relationships. Turns out, results and relationships are intertwined, even inseparable. First of all, there is quite a disconnect between how well leaders believe they are communicating with others and external reviews of their communication. A study found that 92 percent of managers rated themselves as doing an "excellent" or "good" job of managing employees, whereas only 67 percent of those reporting to the same managers agreed. Therefore, it is no surprise that managers dedicate an average of seven or more hours a week to sorting out personality conflicts.[8]

Time lost through conflicts and poor communication leads to lower employee retention and lost revenue. Investing time to establish clear communication channels eliminates a slew of headaches down the road.

 Flex!

You're in the spotlight, so make a conscious effort to be consistently friendly, open, and positive. At the same time, pushing people past their perceived limits is the management version of tough love and yields a stronger, more motivated team.

P.S. You have the resources you need to accomplish your goals.

CHAPTER SEVEN

Being Bossy

A good chief gives, he does not take.

—Mohawk proverb

Boss. Sounds so bossy.
Do this, not that . . . I'll do it.
When's my vacation?

(A haiku, in case you missed that artistic point.)

Carl Jung's book *Memories, Dreams, Reflections* (1961) has an excerpt from a conversation between Jung and Ochwiay Biano, chief of the Taos Pueblo in New Mexico:

> "We do not understand [the whites]. We think that they are mad."

> I asked him why he thought the whites were all mad.

> "They say that they think with their heads," he replied.

> "Why of course. What do you think with?" I asked him in surprise.

> "We think here," he said, indicating his heart.[9]

Chief Biano describes how it is between feelers and thinkers. In particular, people on extreme ends of the spectrum believe those on the other end are mad. To manage effectively, we must set biases aside and learn to appreciate and benefit from differences.

Another disconnect frequently exists between how frontline workers perceive management and the real challenges of managing. Listen to what I was told the other day by a technician in a global securities company:

> **"At some point I'd like to get an easy, no-stress job. Like being a manager."**

Yeah, yeah, I know that makes your blood boil. Don't fret. I stood up for you then and there.

There is a chasm between perceptions and realities. It is not uncommon for those who have never been a manager to view such a position as cushy. Why, the manager doesn't seem to have to do anything. Just hangs out all day in a decent office and surfs the Web. Everyone else does the real work, right? Right? Anybody still out there . . . ?

If managing is so easy, why do so many of us hate it? Because there is a disconnect between what the untrained eye sees as "management" and the actual demands that come with the territory.

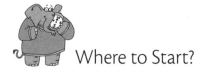

Where to Start?

How about with yourself? Hold yourself accountable for continual improvement and lifelong learning. To be a role model, realize how far you have to go. Set regular goals, put a structure in place to meet them, and evaluate yourself regularly.

How do you know if you did something wrong at work? That's easy! Someone—generally a supervisor of some kind—draws your attention to the fact that you messed up. And how do you know if you did something right?

I'm waiting.

If you are in the same situation as many others, the answer is, You don't. Or, rather, no one seems to notice. Doing things right is a nonevent.

Upshots of this *Pop! Goes the Feedback* include:

1. Poor communication is fertile ground for the creation of rumors.

2. When only negative feedback is provided, productivity is weak.

Lack of communication is often due to the mere fact that many managers are overwhelmed with their duties. A major challenge in managing others is summed up nicely by an associate director at a midsized nonprofit:

Before becoming a manager my deliverable was my performance. While I am still responsible for everything in my own portfolio, I'm also responsible for eight other people. My deliverable now includes everyone else's performance, too. Regardless of my own portfolio and deadlines, I must still be available to, and ultimately responsible for, my team.

Jumpin' Thru Hoops

Clarify Choices

Think of behavior that limits your success. We are going to apply the CCC model: change, consequence, and contract.

Sample limiting behaviors include:

- Starting activities and not following up
- Shouting at others when you are under pressure
- Putting yourself down when you are complimented
- Interrupting others midsentence

My limiting behavior is: _____

Changing my behavior would be beneficial for these reasons:

1.
2.
3.

The **consequences** of making this change include:

1.
2.
3.

Finally, wrap things up with a contract. A contract is a clearly stated (and written!) statement of intention about next steps and goals.

The **contract** I am making with myself for working on this behavior for 30 days is: _____

_____

_____

CCC provides a structure to identify and eliminate limiting behaviors. This model is also a useful tool when providing feedback to others.

Pop! Goes the Feedback

There are few things I cherish more than making a big mess, so this activity is a blast. Literally.

Participants work in groups and are tasked with giving "acceptable" balloons to their boss. "Bosses," randomly selected participants, are told they cannot speak during the duration of the activity. Additionally, bosses are each provided with a safety pin and informed this is the tool for the single type of feedback allowed—they are to pop balloons that do not meet the stringent criteria for acceptability. Acceptable balloons

- must be handed—not thrown, tossed, or bounced—to the boss;
- must be a different color than the one previously presented to the boss;
- must be given to the boss by someone other than the person who presented the previous balloon; and
- must be blown up and tied (any size is fine).

The teams know none of this. The only instructions the team receives are "Get as many balloons accepted by your boss as possible. The team with the most balloons accepted receives a prize."

The teams have no idea what's going on. It gets pretty entertaining for observers. Teams come up with crazy theories. Stuff like one time a team member happened to scratch his head right before handing over an accepted balloon. The team jumped on this as evidence that a head scratch was required and made a mandatory self-enforced rule that everyone had to do this before approaching the boss.

After about ten minutes of general chaos, I ask the teams what criteria they believe were needed for accepted balloons. The lists are unbelievable. They invariably come up with much more detailed theories than the actual restrictions.

This activity is a metaphor for what happens when teams receive negative, inadequate communication. Without positive reinforcement or clear direction, teams compensate by inventing rules with no basis in reality, starting rumors about what management really wants, producing at subpar levels, or just giving up.

Juggling the management of others and your additional job responsibilities requires efficiency. That means providing clear expectations and promoting independence. Introducing...

ERSA!

This lovely acronym stands for

- **E**xpectation
- **R**elinquish
- **S**upport
- **A**ccountable

EXPECTATIONS

Set **expectations** immediately with any new hire and upon the start of any project or assignment. It is alarming how frequently expectations are not clear, time is wasted, work must be redone, and the employee is blamed for falling short.

RELINQUISH

Get out of the way. Promote independence by **relinquishing** the need to be overly involved in your teams' work. Believe me, they will appreciate it, and you will save valuable time and energy.

SUPPORT

Let others know you are there for them as a sounding board, **support** system, and advisor. Supporting your team includes giving them credit for their contributions in front of others, protecting them from external demands and critiques, and jumping in to help out when they're in a crunch.

ACCOUNTABLE

The bookend to setting expectations is holding people **accountable** for the end product. The process of getting there is their choice and might be very different from your own approach. That's fine. You were clear about objectives and provided support. Holding people accountable for their results is critical. If you don't, who will?

Feedback for Managers
Who Hate Giving Feedback

A direct report is driving you out of your skull. You are exhausted, with the weight of the world on your shoulders. You have so many balls in the air you could land a premier solo act at Cirque du Soleil. You don't have a nanosecond to yourself. If you're a T, you're annoyed. If you are an F, you feel guilty for anything and everything.

And your direct report just doesn't get it. Not that he cares.

Sample Example
The Powers of Positive Reinforcement

Myriad compelling studies investigate the remarkable impact of providing positive reinforcement. In particular, comparisons between reprimanding poor performance and reinforcing all-star behaviors point to superior results for the latter tactic. I've read with rapt attention articles proving this again and again, with subjects ranging from various animals to, well, husbands. Why don't you do a little research and see what you drum up?

Let's say you profess, "I'm not good at praising people. It's not my thing. It would seem fake." Consider this little story that happened to me on a business trip.

Traveling for business is a potentially golden opportunity to see places I might not otherwise visit. On the flip side, I end up spending virtually all of my time inside hotels and conference centers. For this reason, I like to take at least one run around the area to get a feel for my fleeting habitat.

Once I was running on a path alongside a city river and happened upon the best graffiti I've ever seen.

First, I noticed, spray painted right on the path itself, "Run faster!" I did as instructed.

A few minutes later, I saw on the ground in front of me "Keep it up!" I did.

Then, "You're doing great!"

I began to look forward to upcoming spray-painted words of encouragement. I was running faster and was now smiling, too. This continued for a few miles.

At one point I started laughing aloud at myself. I realized I was being encouraged anonymously by a (minor) criminal who had never met me, by words not even directed at me. And yet there I was, exceeding my previous pace and feeling notably more upbeat and invigorated.

Any positive reinforcement you provide as a manager has got to beat that—anonymous, vague graffiti. I mean, really. That's a low bar.

So you need to provide feedback. This is a primo example of flexing your style. Let's say you are a hot F. And the report is a flaming T. And you do not flex your style. On Friday you requested a meeting with your employee to discuss "productivity issues," so he knows something is up. You mulled over the situation all weekend and it is now Monday morning. The feedback session goes something like this . . .

Advanced Decoder:

U = You
E = Employee

(Take 1)

U: Hi! How was your weekend?
E: Um, fine.

U: Did you do anything fun?
E: Nope, not really. [Translation: Why are you asking me that?]

U: [Fake laugh.] Me neither. Good weather, though!
E: Yup. [Getting freaked out.]

U: So. I really like having you on my team. You're so much fun and everyone loves having you around.
E: . . .

U: You've got a great smile and make everyone laugh.
E: . . .

U: Okay. So. There are a few issues we need to address.

CUT!

There is no sense going any further with this. It's just too painful. In your effort to establish positive rapport with your T staffer you've accomplished *precisely the opposite.* He is totally frustrated with the flow of this meeting. He is thinking, "Why doesn't she cut to the chase? This is wasting my time."

Now, let's say you've made an earnest attempt to flex your style.

As a skilled, flexible F manager, you know how to yank a slew of T verbiage out of your back pocket on demand.

(Take 2)

U: Hi, Dave. How's it goin'?
E: It's cool.

U: Thanks for meeting with me on a Monday morning. As I mentioned Friday, I want to discuss some performance issues with you.
E: Yeah.

U: I appreciate all your hard work. At the same time, I know there is room for improvement in these three areas . . .

CUT!

This, my friend, is flexing your style.

For an F employee, this approach wouldn't fly. He'd feel attacked already. Yet a strong T is down with it. He is glad you are on task. The Platinum Rule upgrades "Treat others how you want to be treated" to "Treat others how *they* want to be treated."[10] Plenty of people you manage don't want to be treated in remotely the same way you want to be treated. Tailor how you interact with others to their style, not yours.

The following feedback guidelines hold for both Ts and Fs.

Do!	Don't!
Focus on what's right	Focus on what's wrong
Phrase feedback positively	Emphasize what NOT to do
Give feedback regularly	Wait for an annual review
Be specific	Be vague
Challenge to excel	Sugarcoat

So, for instance, after a board meeting where your staffer Stephanie has presented a new marketing campaign, consider replacing this:

[Calling across the room as people are filing out.] Hey, Steph, over here! Was that for real? Next time, please at least make sure the AV is up and running before the top dogs file in! Nothing breaks credibility like not knowing how to advance a slide on a brand-new projector. Whatever, you picked it up halfway. Next time, maybe more oomph, though, okay? Let's cover the details at your performance review next month. Anything we need to talk about now? I have to fly to my next appointment; you went a few minutes over.

with this:

[In Stephanie's office, ten minutes after her board presentation.] Hi, Stephanie. Congratulations on your first delivery of the new campaign. I was impressed by how you handled that tough Q & A in the last few minutes, especially when the client asked about the source of the market research study you cited and you knew off the cuff! I realized we need to get you a tutorial on our new AV equipment. Let's prioritize that this week. Your presentations will get better each time. Can you take a few minutes to reflect on what you want to work on? We'll address those areas when we meet this afternoon?

Even trickier is modifying feedback to match temperaments. It's worth the effort. The better you get at this, the easier managing becomes.

Feelers usually prefer . . .	Thinkers usually prefer . . .
Being eased into performance appraisals	Going straight into content of appraisals
Discussion	Direct advice
Meaningful feedback	Pragmatic feedback
Being motivated by purpose	Being motivated by results

Just in case, let's clear up any misperception that Ts somehow don't care about receiving accolades for good performance. This rumor can often be traced back to Ts themselves claiming they don't need that sort of thing. Don't believe them. What they disdain is flowery, overly effusive praise, which they deem inauthentic. However, even the T with the toughest persona in your office secretly appreciates meaningful, specific, positive reinforcement. Just don't overdo it. With Ts, less is more.

Your Part of the Bargain

What type of example do you set for others? What work environment do you promote? Beware of two gory green workplace monsters: criticizing and complaining.

For starters, resist the urge to judge people. You're always, always wrong when you do. Always. Did I mention you're never right when

Jumpin' Thru Hoops

PROD: A Feedback Structure for All

All you have do is **prod** your folks a bit. Simple stuff.

1. **P!** State the *problem:* _____

_____

_____

2. **R!** Clarify the desired *result:* _____

_____

_____

3. **O!** Say what you objectively *observe:* _____

_____

_____

4. **D!** What would you like to be *different?* _____

_____

_____

you pass judgment? Sure, you know right from wrong; that's how you got where you are today! That's not the issue. The disconnect kicks in when you aren't inside someone else's head and life 24/7. You might just miss a few important points. Like what really happened or why a person made a decision that you could never possibly understand. I could go on forever. Instead, let's just agree that passing judgment isn't the way to go.

Plus it leads, inevitably, to chitchat. Gossip. You know the drill. Like junk food that ends up tasting like cardboard. So-o-o not worth it. The second you finish chowing you realize your mistake, and there is no going back.

Criticism isn't at all the same as providing useful constructive feedback, by the way. The skill of meaningful feedback is a valuable tool of superior managers. Criticism = judgment. The purpose of criticizing others is to insult them. The purpose of providing feedback is to improve them.

The second gory green monster of the workplace is complaining. Few traits are less appealing than a person who continually comments on what's wrong. Okay, maybe loud gum chewing.

How about making "No complaining!" a guiding principle of your leadership practice. Why not? Go wild.

Don't complain. Or as they say in the old country, no kvetching. Isn't that a heck of a word?

Sociopaths and You

Almost everyone you manage means well. It's that pesky *almost* we'll address briefly here. One in twenty-five people is a sociopath, meaning they function without a conscience. Normal methods of communication don't work with them. Sociopathy is a social disorder recognized in DSM-IV and is not limited to easily identifiable stereotypes. The lovely news is that out of every hundred people you encounter on the job, ninety-six are fundamentally good people muddling through, just like you. You can figure out the other side of this equation without my help.

If you think you may be entwined with someone initially compelling who leaves a path of destruction, there are excellent books on the topic (a few are included in "Relevant Reads" at the back of this one). As a manager, it is important to be aware of this disorder and to be alert. Give people the benefit of the doubt; statistics favor the possibility that a difficult workplace relationship is a reconcilable challenge. Don't just throw in the towel. Keep in mind the experience of an owner of a midsized restaurant chain:

> We almost fired an employee because she wasn't performing. Instead, we sat down together and I explained exactly what I expected. She completely improved the quality of her work. If we had fired her it would have been a terrible injustice and real failure on my part.

Work hard, reserve judgment, don't jump the gun. At the same time, a prime management skill is the ability to realize when to stop pouring energy and effort into an unmanageable individual. If nothing has worked, do some research. Among other sundry features, sociopaths are entirely without empathy (although they can fake it) and have the added charm of not being weighed down with normal human feelings. Untangling, detaching, and when possible, disengaging entirely are the only solutions. Chances are high at some point you will encounter a sociopath and different rules apply.

Flex!

Flexing your feedback to fit the recipient's personality is the best way to achieve lasting results.

P.S. If what you're doing isn't working, try something else.

CHAPTER EIGHT

Don't Cry in My Office . . .
I Have a Deadline to Meet

Everything I know about management was learned "on the job" by playing in

rock and roll bands. Compared to arguing with angry, intoxicated drummers,

pretty much anything you run into in the workplace is a piece of cake.

—Laurence Biely

Drip drip drip go tears
Rolling, your cheek to my desk
Blurring memo ink

(Another haiku . . . I'm going through a phase.)

Perhaps you have found yourself in the surprise, unadvertised role of staff therapist. You are not alone. It happens to the best of us. Dealing with people's emotions poses unique challenges for thinker and feeler managers.

THINKER CHALLENGE EXAMPLE

You believe people need to check emotions at the door. Business isn't personal, and people must behave professionally. Nevertheless, emotionally charged conflicts regularly crop up among your staff.

FEELER CHALLENGE EXAMPLE

People flock to you with their emotional issues, draining your energy. You try to help, yet you overidentify, take on their problems, and lose productive work time.

Whether you're a T or an F, you are bound to come face to face with employees' emotions on a regular basis.

I'm Not a Psychologist, I Just Play One at Work

Here are a few tips to manage your side job as staff psychologist.

When someone asks if you have time to talk and it's not a true-blue emergency, tell him you have ten minutes. During this time, give him your complete attention. When ten minutes are over, wrap it up. It's far better to give your full attention for a previously disclosed short time frame than to provide partial attention for an hour, hoping he'll take the hint.

If a staff member is agitated, reflect back his feelings, with validating comments such as "Sounds like that was very upsetting for you." Saying, "Don't feel that way" or "It's not so bad" will only make him feel de-validated and misunderstood.

Ask what he thinks will improve the situation. Let him brainstorm his own solutions. At the end of the (brief!) conversation, recap what the person said he would do about the issue.

If a person is visibly agitated, request that he sit down. Psychologists have found that people become calmer when seated.

If an employee is upset with you, repeat back what he says specifically upset him. This shows you are listening empathetically and reduces the edge.

In the case of a recurring or serious situation, refer the person to human resources.

Use a neutral yet caring tone that appropriately matches your visitor's manner. If he is speaking softly, you do too. If he is animated, show energy yourself. Matching tone helps build rapport, especially when someone is upset.

Be empathetic without getting drawn into his emotions. Overidentifying with his angst or frustration accelerates tension and decreases your effectiveness.

Listen to the people around you. Heed this management advice from the CEO of a multilocation car dealership known for award-winning customer service:

Lead with questions. And listen to the person giving the answers. You've already lost if you think you know the answers.

Asking questions saves you from jumping in to "solve" others' challenges. Well-formed questions also redirect attention from mulling over a problem to identifying a solution.

Save Me from Myself

When I was in my twenties I volunteered at crisis hotlines in a couple of U.S. metropolitan areas. A match made in heaven. Feelers with time on their hands are drawn to this work like ants to a tasty picnic. De-lec-ta-ble. Gather a group of idealistic feelers in a secret location—generally a basement without windows and with twenty-year-old couches—provide them with outdated phones and let them save the world, one stressed-out, anonymous caller at a time.

Yet there's a catch.

Working a crisis hotline is serious business because lives are at stake. Training is required. The consequence of the training is that a group of save-the-world feelers is taught to behave like off-the-chart thinkers. What a brilliant trick.

One time I answered the phone and said the standard, "Crisis hotline. May I help you?"

The response: "I sure hope so, because I'm going to kill myself."

When I recount this in a presentation, I pause and ask the group how they believe a feeler would react to such a statement. Standard guesses are along these lines:

- "Oh, no! Don't do it."
- [Sob uncontrollably]
- "But life is worth living!"
- [Break into a cold sweat]
- "Please don't kill yourself."
- [Panic]

Nope. Being a well-trained little hotliner, I responded matter-of-factly: "Okay. How do you plan on killing yourself?"

As I tell this story, shock waves reverberate throughout the room as feelers gasp in noisy, judgmental unison. How could I be so cruel, so heartless, so unfeeling?

And my feeler readers, despite a highly prized moral fiber, are now wondering if the spine of this book is too creased to prevent a refund.

I will say this about thinkers: They are beautifully practical. Crisis hotlines train volunteers to respond as thinkers to a suicide threat because the next step in the conversation is entirely different if the response is "I have a gun pointed to my head and I'm ready to shoot" than it is if the caller says, "I dunno. I was thinking maybe about pills."

Only by applying a hard-core thinker technique could I successfully help save this guy's life. Sometimes we need to learn the behaviors of our own opposite to accomplish what matters to us the most.

Positive Outcomes

I hate the pressure of always feeling like I need to have the answers to solve everyone's problems.

—Line manager in a clothing manufacturing firm

We can rename "problems" as "challenges," if we want to be progressive about it. I heard that Mother Teresa banned anyone in her path from saying the word *problem*, insisting they replace it with *gift*. So conversations allegedly went something like this: "Mother Teresa, I have a very large gift to tell you about . . ."

I apparently have not reached the ethereal heights of Mother Teresa. Because, for example, if a client cancels a major project the day before launch, I call that a definite problem. Furthermore, when approached by others with problems, most of us ask a certain type of question. Here are examples of what are called problem-based questions:

- What's wrong?
- Why do you have this problem?
- What or who caused it?
- What is the impact of the problem?
- How has this problem limited your success?

There's nothing wrong with these questions. They are useful in two main ways: They enable us to learn about the problem, and they allow the person with the problem to let off steam. That's about it.

Problem-based questions don't move anything forward. Take a closer look. They all focus on the past—what happened, why, and how much harm has been done. When we concentrate on what already happened, we release responsibility and lose control.

Once you understand the gist of a problem, there is no reason whatsoever to dwell there. And guess what? There is a whole different way to ask questions, with an outcome-based approach. Outcome questions lead us from the problem into possibilities.

Get a load of these:

- What do you want?

- What will this get you? (or) What do you *really* want?

- What progress have you already made?

- What are possible ways to resolve this challenge?

- What is a step toward achieving your desired outcome?

Outcome questions focus on future possibilities, directing our attention toward options, choices, and responsibility.

Outcome questions direct attention toward achievable outcomes. They improve performance and attitude while empowering your direct reports to resolve their own problems. They let you off the hook in the most appropriate way.

Problem-Based Questions	Outcome-Based Questions
Explore limitations	Explore possibilities
Delve into the problem	Identify solutions
Focus on what has already occurred	Focus on what can occur
Highlight past events	Highlight future possibilities
Emphasize lack of control	Emphasize choice
Highlight what's wrong	Highlight what you *really* want

My favorite question (Well, second favorite. Right after "Do you want fries with that?") is

"What do you want?"

Let's call this the *Down To It* question. Because more than any other question I know, it gets people down to the core of a matter.

Make the *Down To It* your go-to tool to help people resolve their predicaments. This question is unbelievably versatile. Although be careful. "What do you *want*?" is miles away from "What do *you* want?"

Tone is king. It always matters when communicating; however, it makes a particular difference with this question. Play around. Say the *Down To It* aloud as if you're annoyed, harried, empathetic. Hear what I mean? Sincerity relies on tone. Now apologize to the fellow red-eye travelers you just woke up.

Sample Example

I Want...

I used to work as a caseworker for an ABC TV consumer advocacy program. Some situations were life or death, whereas others, although maddening, were less severe.

One consumer phoned to tell me that she had hired a company to install new carpet in her condo while she was at work. She returned to discover they had covered her entire home in the wrong carpet. She was livid.

What was the obvious next step for me to resolve this issue? To contact the carpet company for a job redo, right? Wrong. Instead, I asked what seems to be a gratuitous question with an obvious answer. You guessed it: "What do you want?"

My question took my caller aback. She hesitated as she processed the question and prepared her answer.

"I want . . . I want . . . an apology!" Those were her exact words. Followed by, "This carpeting isn't so bad. I'll just keep it."

All I could think was how much easier my day had just become because of the *Down To It* question.

I observe managers overpromise and overdeliver because they make offers rather than inquiries. When someone says she is overwhelmed with an assignment, the well-meaning manager often reacts by offering to help rather than asking, "What do you want?" Sometimes the answer is the employee just wanted to let off some steam so she can get back to tackling the work.

When a potential new customer requests a proposal, the typical response is along the lines of "I will get it to you by the close of business" rather than "When would you like the proposal?" (a variation on "What do you want?").

If you ever feel overextended, do yourself a big favor and start asking people what they want rather than making the assumption you already know.

You're Fired!

Sometimes I separate clients into Ts and Fs and give the two groups identical assignments: "You have to fire someone on your team. What do you do?"

I have done this activity with hundreds of people and the responses are incredibly consistent. The Fs sigh heavily and lament, "We thought this was supposed to be fun," while simultaneously the Ts crack jokes about not letting the door hit you on the way out. Then the two teams get to work discussing the assignment, summarizing their points on a whiteboard to share with the entire group later.

One day I had a group working on the assignment. Take a look at the Fs' list:

- Stress out
- Feel guilty
- Assure him I really like him as a person
- Tell him how bad I feel
- Remind him of all his great traits
- Say it isn't because of something he did wrong
- Recall good times we had and that I'd be there for him
- Offer to be a reference

Notice how many feeling words there are—virtually every bullet point has a feeling-based comment or word. One T quipped, "I would think I was being promoted, not fired!"

Meanwhile, the Ts came up with the following:

- Have a witness
- Fire on a Friday
- Have written documentation that we both sign
- Tell them specifically why they are being fired

- Give them severance information

- Be objective and nonemotional

Upon hearing this list, one F (who happened to also be an introvert) couldn't take it anymore. She jumped up and said indignantly, "How would you like to be fired that way?!"

Major moment.

A T (also female, as it so happened) said calmly, "This is exactly the way I would like to be fired."

The Ts are not a bunch of cold-hearted meanies. They were firing someone in a pragmatic, logical way . . . the same way they themselves want to be treated. So if Ts are managing Ts, all is well organically. Likewise if Fs are managing Fs. Quite often, though, as you might surmise, this is not the case. Ts are supervising Fs and Fs are overseeing Ts all over the place. You can imagine the potential for some messy situations.

That is, unless managers employ the Platinum Rule introduced earlier. The Platinum Rule mandates treating others not as *we* want to be treated but as each particular employee wants to be treated. I recommend the ancient system of asking people what motivates them. Use that as a guide.

The rub is that to succeed at flexing your style you must hone the dual skill set of capturing subtle data about how others like to be treated (if you're not in a position to ask directly) and matching your behavior to other people's preferences. Takes practice, though definitely doable and pays off!

I must point out there is no evidence that Ts or Fs are better qualified to fire (or hire) employees. They simply have different approaches. The most effective leaders are Ts *and* Fs skilled at flexing their style. When firing, you may never see that person again. In other workplace situations, however, such as annual reviews, you will continue to interact, so flexing your style is arguably even more critical.

Jumpin' Thru Hoops

Filter, Filter

I love this little activity. To achieve the desired effect, you must be disciplined. Follow my rules. Disregard your base instincts to cheat, lie, and steal.

1. Take ten seconds, give or take a second, to read the following sentence:

FEATURE FILMS ARE THE RESULT OF YEARS OF STUDY AND FORMAL YEARS OF EXPERIMENTS.

2. Now, cover it up with your hand, piece of paper, or whatever. Do as instructed and nobody will get hurt.
3. Next, think back on the sentence and write down how many Fs it contains.
4. Last step: Look at the sentence again for ten seconds, cover it up, and revise your response.

Most people don't notice all six Fs in the first reading. There is a reason for this besides carelessness: Our brains are designed to sort and filter data for perceived importance, and we have certain criteria, many of them subconscious, for what is "important." First letters of nouns and adjectives, for example. So you most likely recollected the Fs in *feature* and *films*. Little connector words (Prepositions perhaps? Where's a grammar teacher when I need one?) are negligible; we don't dwell upon *of*. That accounts for why those three Fs are overlooked by most first-time readers.

Some people have backgrounds or talents that put them at an advantage for a high success rate at this activity—such as editors or the lucky few with photographic memories.

As the administrator of this activity, I could greatly heighten your success rate by alerting you in advance about why you are reading this sentence, your performance criteria, and how success will be measured. If I were a helpful person, I would have said, "Today's assignment is to read a single sentence. Resources are tight, so you can only allot ten seconds to this task. However, what the sentence says is unimportant. I want you to direct your attention only to counting the number of times the letter F appears. Remember to pay attention to all the words, not just the nouns, and note that Fs also appear in small words."

Helping staff know what to filter dissipates frustration and heightens success.

And One More Thing

When motivating others, remember to state things in the positive. We can't *not* do something; we can only do something. For instance, researchers—gotta love them—discovered that when kids are told, "Don't color on the walls," what they actually hear is "Color on the walls!" So remember to motivate through positive statements.

 Flex!

Expand your inquiry style to incorporate outcome-based questions. You'll help others resolve their own challenges: building resilience, confidence, and independence.

P.S. There's always another choice.

CHAPTER NINE

Inside, Outside, Upside Down

If you smile when you are alone, then you really mean it.
—Andy Rooney

Introverts crave one on one
Extroverts party, lots of fun
Intros think before they talk
Extros speak before they've thought
Extros go wide, intros deep
Managing these folks is quite a feat.

I've been informed by my readers that you want to chat about how our other favorite personality dimension—introversion and extroversion—affects management style.

Voilà! This chapter appears before your very eyes. Please submit your second and third wishes in writing, in triplicate.

Let's start by asserting there is no correlation between Thinking–Feeling and Extroversion–Introversion. However, the various combinations (four, to be precise) of these two dimensions certainly impact how we manage. The introverted feeler is going to be the most sensitive and introspective of the possible combinations, for example. An extroverted thinker is most likely to inadvertently offend others with his characteristically blunt communication. The extroverted feeler is most prone to organize birthday pizza lunches. An introverted thinker is most likely to work in, well, IT! (Get it? That's the abbreviation of introverted thinker! Plus, it fits.)

The following charts excerpted from *Networking for People Who Hate Networking* will help you wrap your head around the distinguishing features of introverts and extroverts.[11]

Introverts	Extroverts
Think to talk	*Talk to think*
Go deep	*Go wide*
Energize alone	*Energize with others*
Reflective	Verbal
Focused	Expansive
Self-reliant	Social

Networking Preferences

Listening	Speaking
Calm	Activity
One-on-one	Groups

Networking Strategies

Introverts	Extroverts
1. Pause (Research)	1. Patter (Discuss)
2. Process (Focus)	2. Promote (Sell)
3. Pace (Restore)	3. Party (Socialize)

The Moment of Truth!
Extrovert versus Introvert Managers

Dueling truisms from both villages:

Extroverts	Introverts
The more the merrier	Less is more
The whole is greater than the sum of its parts	Groups slow things down

When I've asked extroverts and introverts about the ups and downs of being a manager, here are some verbatim responses.

EXTROVERTS' FAVORITE PARTS OF MANAGING

- "Interacting with lots of people." (*Extroverted feeler*)

- "Open, constant communication. Better to overcommunicate." (*Extroverted feeler*)

- "Developing people and building together." (*Extroverted thinker*)

- "Don't be afraid to disclose your weaknesses to your team." (*Extroverted thinker*)

INTROVERTS' FAVORITE PARTS OF MANAGING

- "Reflection on own practice regularly." (*Introverted feeler*)

- "Coaching individuals to facilitate their success. (*Introverted feeler*)

- "Developing direct reports to be independent and self-sufficient." (*Introverted thinker*)

- "Keep listening to people. After explaining your goals, ask open-ended questions." (*Introverted thinker*)

Regarding differences of opinion, introverts are more likely to trip up by internalizing their perceptions, not checking them against reality, and stewing over conflict longer than necessary. Extroverts are more likely to immediately share their disagreements and criticisms verbally with others before fully processing their ideas internally.

Whether working through a conflict or simply reviewing the week's tasks, schedule a bit of extra time for meetings with extroverts. They will appreciate it, and you'll make up the time in meetings with introverts.

Introvert Central

I was presenting at a conference composed of research professionals specializing in statistical analysis. They took a personality assessment, and I was astonished to find myself awash in a sea of seventy introverts. Not a sole extrovert among them!

Lest you be working through residual stereotypes, this was not a quiet group. They were downright giddy. The word *ruckus* comes to mind.

We had a blast.

Near the end of the session I confided that they were the first group (larger than a team of four or five people) I'd worked with that was composed entirely of self-identified introverts. They were unimpressed. As one pointed out, "Would anyone ever even publically admit to being an extrovert?" Others bobbed their heads up and down in enthusiastic introvert agreement.

Communication is, of course, a massive component of managing. A hasty assumption is that, by definition, extroverts are better communicators than introverts. This is hooey.

Introverted and extroverted managers communicate differently—each camp has strengths, go-to styles, and challenges. As with thinkers and feelers, neither introverts nor extroverts have cornered the market on best management practices.

What works for you is your customized best approach.

And what strategies do extroverts and introverts use when they inherit a new team? Here's what I was told by specimens from each side of the fence.

Extrovert: "I get to know the people who report to me and help them get to know me."

Introvert: "I demonstrate that I respect their space and privacy while letting them know how to reach me."

Let's make it tidy . . .

	Natural Strengths	Go-To Style	Self-Identified Challenges
Introvert Managers	■ Listening ■ Picking up on subtle cues ■ Getting at deeper, initially hidden issues	■ One-on-one meetings ■ Individual contribution to group projects ■ "Let me know if you need me"	■ Contributing to group discussion ■ Attending meetings ■ Firing people ■ Interruptions
Extrovert Managers	■ Inclusiveness ■ Generating ideas verbally ■ Organizing group events	■ Get everyone's input ■ Teamwork ■ Lots of meetings	■ Working late alone on projects ■ Focusing on one item or person ■ Overscheduling ■ Not befriending direct reports

And now! True confessions from real live extrovert managers! If this doesn't beat Ripley's Believe It or Not, I don't know what does. Self-professed challenges for extrovert leaders:

- "I find it easy to get sucked into the chaos and not think things through. This sets us all up for a rocky time."
- "The loneliness of the buck-stops-here decision making."
- "I still want to be one of the gang. I feel left out."

It's only fair to follow these with true confessions of introverts. Normally it is difficult to get introverts to reveal their inner thoughts unless we are well acquainted. Somehow, I managed.

- "I'll admit, I will sometimes just e-mail people down the hall to avoid talking face to face."
- "Having to say good morning to everyone I pass in the halls is tedious and draining!"
- "I just can't live with an open-door policy. Being interrupted all day completely throws me off."

When you hear someone espouse the "management by walking around" system, you can bet your bottom dollar that person is an extrovert (unless they mean "walking around outside . . . alone"). If you are an introvert, don't do it! It just won't work for you. That doesn't mean being a grump or a hermit. It means smiling confidently and warmly at people you pass in the hallway but not spending a third of your workday schmoozing. You will deflate faster than a balloon with a hole. Pop! Where'd you go?

If you are an extrovert, do your walk-around thing. With the caveat that you notice and honor the needs of introverts, for whom maybe a smile and wave will suffice. If you are an introvert, you don't get to hide behind a closed door all day. However, you are allowed to close it for times requiring particular concentration. It is what you need to do your job.

Go, go, go. That's the manager's life. What to do? Depends on who you are. Remember: Introverts energize alone; extroverts energize with others. To refuel at lunch, extroverts can hang out with friends; introverts can open a delicious book. The challenges vary. While spending time with subordinates is not entirely off-limits, a supervisor can't treat these relationships the same way as friendships outside the workplace. That is a particular challenge of the extrovert manager. For introverts, the challenge is appearing too standoffish—you never seem to join the team at pizza lunches. Maybe go once in a while. It won't kill you.

Speaking of which, organizing occasional events for teammates to hang out together is a real morale booster, whether off-site or with a simple potluck. I highly recommend kicking it off with some structured activities. Even going around and having people share some nonwork-related accomplishment from the past year, or a favorite recipe, or a hidden talent, or any number of other conversation openers. Contrary to popular—misinformed!—belief, introverts do better with structured than unstructured events.

Jumpin' Thru Hoops

Introverts and Extroverts at Work

If you manage (or are on) a team, there's a splendid chance you've got a selection of introverts and extroverts on hand.

Envelopes is a problem-solving technique that stimulates collaboration between introverts and extroverts, to address workplace challenges.

Ask your team a few days before you convene what they perceive to be challenges (hot topics) currently facing the group as a whole. Allow them a few days in advance to ponder, compile, and submit their ideas. Ideas can be submitted anonymously, too.

Guide the participants to issues over which they have a reasonable amount of control, *not* matters such as

- a changing policy of the overseas parent company;
- unpredictable weather patterns;
- the incompetent department down the hall; or
- slashed resources due to financial losses.

Instead, useful hot topics to consider are along the lines of

- inconsistent communication channels among coworkers;
- lack of collaboration within the department;
- confusion over job delineation;
- differing opinions about where the team is headed; or
- inability to quantify the team's contribution to the parent company.

Notice that the first list is outer-directed and the second is inner-directed. This second list focuses on patterns, behaviors, and responsibilities of the team itself.

Call everyone together for a one-hour meeting. Set up four table groups and stick to the time frame—this wins over everybody, even the extroverts. In advance, ask an extrovert (an extroverted feeler, perhaps?) to lead everyone in a five- to ten-minute team activity. Share a summary of the submitted hot topics and apply the technique of multivoting (see chapter 6) to narrow it down to the top four.

Participants get to pick which of the four hot topics to work on, separating by tables. Each table has an envelope with one of the hot topics written on the outside and three index cards inside.

The envelopes are passed clockwise, so now each group has another team's hot topic in front of them. Teams take out one of the index cards and get one minute to brainstorm initial ideas for that topic. When the minute is up, the index cards go back into the envelopes, the envelopes are passed again, and teams repeat what they just did for a second topic. This pattern continues three times, until the groups' original hot topics have returned to their rightful table, now with three index cards of ideas inside. That whole segment takes less than five minutes.

Now the teams work in earnest for twenty to thirty minutes. They can review, use, and/or discard the other teams' quickly generated suggestions, which serve the primary purpose of seeding the discussion. Now teams discuss their hot topic in more depth, generating a few recommendations for initial actions to address their topic.

Each team makes a three-minute presentation summarizing their initial recommended actions. The group collectively discusses the results, asks questions, makes suggestions, and decides on next steps.

Envelopes is an efficient, high-energy method of tackling shared challenges. It is designed to combine the strengths of both introverts and extroverts, resulting in effective collaboration.

Tricks of the Trade

Up next are two quick, useful techniques for managing introverts and extroverts. Although first we have myths to dispel.

MYTH 1: INTROVERTS ARE NEGATIVE

While untrue, this erroneous belief is understandable. What are its origins? Because introverts think to talk, when presented with a new idea, frequently their first reaction is to say no. This tendency earns them the unenviable labels of *negative* and *stubborn.* In reality, they are just protecting the need to speak before agreeing to something. Introverts require time to process new ideas.

SOLUTION

Luckily, there is an easy way to get around this conundrum. Write up your idea. Put it on the aforementioned introvert's desk. Mention you'd like him to look it over, then run away fast. Return at a leisurely pace a few hours later and you may be quite surprised to find a calm, smiling introvert with a few questions about your brilliant new expense submission procedure.

MYTH 2: EXTROVERTS ARE UNRELIABLE

Although also untrue, this erroneous belief is understandable, too! Where does this one spring from? Extroverts talk to think; they speak in order to know what they really believe. What happens? An extrovert on your team states loud and clear his intention to take over a new project and run with it. He never does. So unreliable! Clearly can't be counted on.

Not so fast. What happened is that, early in the meeting, he was thinking aloud about the new project and got caught up in the moment. He was speaking stream-of-consciousness, working through his thoughts by speaking aloud. You believed him *without doing a reality check.*

SOLUTION

Rather than labeling an extrovert staffer as flaky, decide instead to hold yourself accountable for communicating clearly with him. Accept that he processes ideas by talking. Explicitly discuss and agree upon next steps after each discussion.

If someone has a truly deep-rooted aversion to managing others, alternatives include becoming a contractor, entrepreneur, or other solo-based professional (we also discussed self-demotions in chapter 4). However, these options hold much greater appeal for introverts because they thrive on working independently. Extroverts frequently cite loneliness as a major drawback to working alone. They do better looking into alternatives within a larger structure, to maintain a routine sense of community.

 Flex!

Build cohesion among introverts and extroverts by playing to the strengths of both.

P.S. If someone can do it, you can learn it.

CHAPTER TEN

Charisma 'n' You

One kind word can warm three winter months.

—Japanese proverb

I'm not smooth and I'm not cool
I'm not mod, I'm so old-skool
I'm not hip and I'm not hop
My hair's a mess, it's like a mop
I need to be like someone else
. . . unless I can just be my Self.

Perhaps you have heard the term *executive presence*. Maybe you know what it means. I have no idea. I believe it has something to do with when a tall, distinguished-looking man commands a room, steering the conversation around him like an enormous Navy ship. These people, with virtually no characteristics I can personally relate to, are described as having magnetic personalities. That could certainly cause difficulties when traveling through security at airport terminals, but luckily I don't have that problem.

Do you ever feel like a *reverse* magnet? Repelling the crowds effortlessly. The party parts for you like the Red Sea! Pure magic.

Good news. This can all be fixed so you too can attract steel beams straight out of a building's foundation. Real charisma has nothing to do with stature (phew!), gender, age, socioeconomics, or whatever. It has to do with . . . Allow me to demonstrate with a few real-life examples.

We will delve into this chapter by learning about three men in three distinct professions, each of whom I have had the honor to meet personally.

Exhibit A

I lived in a community where garbage needed to be brought to a central compactor for disposal. A man named Mark ran the garbage compactor and recycling operation. Mark managed a staff of four, with virtually no turnover. Mark took it upon himself to operate the compactor himself whenever it was open. Imagine the attitude of someone with this job—standing outside in often-freezing weather, disposing of other people's garbage. It would be understandable if he had a chip on his shoulder and regarded the patrons irritably. Such a guy would greet the customers with a grunt and send them on their way.

Instead, Mark had a spark inside. He did not greet his customers negatively. Instead, he greeted each of us with an upbeat energy that made us laugh and leave happier than when we came . . . not from visiting a four-star restaurant but from disposing of our garbage! Mark joked around with people as we drove up in our warm cars, and said he looked forward to seeing us again when we left.

Here's a guy with plenty to complain about—a thankless outside job and low wages. Yet his treatment of others resulted in many positive relationships. His staff stayed year after year. They soaked in his positivity, which permeated the site. Mark cultivated a special rapport with his patrons and received gifts and warm wishes throughout the year. He described his staff as friendly and personable. A mirror of himself.

One late autumn morning, Mark greeted me characteristically, "What a beautiful day! You'd have to have something really wrong with you to not be happy on a day like today," as he hoisted yet another garbage bag onto the compactor's conveyer belt.

Exhibit B

In a different industry entirely is Antonio, the owner and sole proprietor of a small kitchen design firm. Antonio works day and night and prides himself on exceeding customer expectations. He doesn't complain when he is asked to draw and redraw plans to match a customer's breezy whims, and he never pulls rank with his staff. He manages a diverse team of two dozen employees, from designers to builders. Like Mark, Antonio owes his success to the belief that work isn't work.

Antonio is known to regularly exclaim enthusiastically, "This is fun! Can you imagine doing this for a living?"

Antonio is not the CEO of a Fortune 500 company or independently wealthy. He sits at a well-worn desk on a showroom floor. His workstation is indistinguishable from any of his sales staff's, and casual shoppers could be forgiven for mistaking him for one of the salesmen.

Antonio cannot believe his good luck. He turns vague requests into full-fledged reality, visits work sites daily, and helps haul shipments with his drivers. He believes he enables his clients to reach their dreams. Antonio says he earns a living in a career that allows him to "play" all day.

Exhibit C

Ezekiel is a self-employed shoeshiner. So we can rightly call him an entrepreneur. Ezekiel's job is to kneel down in front of patrons to scrub their shoes 'til they glisten from polish, a well-worn cloth, and his magic touch. His domain is a small shoeshine stand out in front of a row of prestigious shops in Washington, DC. Ezekiel has set up shop there for over twenty years and has a cadre of dedicated, loyal customers.

One sweltering summer afternoon, Ezekiel was happily chatting with the current recipient of a signature shine when a businessperson waiting his turn jokingly ribbed Ezekiel to hurry up.

"Hey, Zeke! Stop your talking and get back to work!"

Without missing a beat or losing his wide grin, Ezekiel quipped, "Work?! When it starts feeling like work, I quit!"

Jumpin' Thru Hoops

Living in the World

Think of someone who seems to have an inner glow. Cheery and upbeat, she or he has a knack for looking on the lighter, brighter side of challenges.

I selected: _____

Because: _____

Behaviors I observe: _____

Characteristics I admire: _____

Now recall a person who seems to exude negativity. He or she is down and out, focusing on the worst.

I selected: _____

Because: _____

Behaviors I observe: _____

Characteristics I notice: _____

Perhaps you have noticed that the first person seems to bring out the best in people. He or she is friendly and positive, and others respond accordingly. The second person, anticipating conflict, creates it.

Make a conscious choice to emulate the characteristics in people you admire.

In reality, Ezekiel is extremely efficient. He focuses on the shoes in front of him as the most important thing in the world. He derives pleasure from excelling at his work, making him a customer magnet.

Coveting the perceived magnetism or presumed good fortune of others is a dead-end street. The fast track to charm is to finding joy in your work (and life). Then you can build your own version of presence that's authentic and lasting.

And from here, the natural leap is to a discussion of . . . lotteries. I know you were thinking the same thing.

Lotteries

Does money buy happiness? The *mature* answer is no. Yet the mind-boggling number of lottery tickets sold shouts a resounding *Yes!*

Even so, studies of lottery winners reveal that, one year after striking it rich, winners return to their previous happiness equilibrium and wind up approximately as satisfied with life as they were before winning millions of dollars.

In 1978 Philip Brickman, a social psychologist at Northwestern University, studied lottery winners just as lotteries were gaining in popularity. His work revealed that lottery winners actually reported lower levels of pleasure from daily activities than did nonlottery winners.

Happiness is relative, marked only by changes from the recent past. Through more expansive studies, Brickman discovered that we adapt to life circumstances, good and bad. After a windfall, the satisfaction fades, replaced by indifference and new striving. Constant adaptation to a cushier lifestyle leads to what he dubbed the hedonic treadmill, as we seek out higher levels of reward to maintain the same subjective pleasure.[12]

This is hard for us regular working folks to swallow, yet sparkling celebrities are endlessly quoted in interviews attesting to the same concept—money and other external rewards do not seem to buy happiness.

The same goes for being promoted to management. I understand your salary didn't take quite the $350 million leap of some lottery winners, yet the concept holds steady. From afar, achieving a promotion to (or within) management seems a ticket toward success. And success leads to fulfillment. And fast on the heels of fulfillment is the mystical world of happiness. Right?

Not so fast.

Everybody in the world is seeking happiness—and there is one sure way to find it. That is by controlling your thoughts. Happiness doesn't depend on outward conditions. It depends on inner conditions.

—Dale Carnegie, *How to Win Friends and Influence People*

Do yourself a favor and listen to Mr. Carnegie. Everybody else does. After all, he's the go-to guy for making friends.

Another study revealed that cultures that place high importance on money and materialism have lower overall levels of well-being. Similar findings hold true for individuals—higher materialism correlates with lower overall happiness.[13]

External factors like acquiring money or promotions don't ultimately infuse us with an inner glow. Our perception of who we are and conviction of what we have to offer is the root of charisma.

What is charisma's allure? What's the desired result? To be admired and respected? If so, there are many paths to the top of the mountain. All require that others sense your authentic passion.

J. J. Frazer is the founder and CEO of New Horizon Security Services, the fastest-growing uniformed security officer company in the United States in 2011. His passion is humility, which he translates into his business model in a very tangible way. Every one of his more than five thousand employees must complete one good deed each day. It's required. He seeks to hire only kind, humble people.

J. J. is creative, passionate, and principled. That's a pretty appealing version of charisma, and his ever-growing, committed staff seems to agree.

 Flex!

To truly shine, focus on what's right, not what's wrong.

P.S. We are in charge of our minds and therefore our results.

CHAPTER ELEVEN

Bonus Track:
This Amp Goes to Eleven![*]

*Treat people as if they were what they ought to be and you help
them to become what they are capable of being.*

—Johann Wolfgang von Goethe

---

* *This Is Spinal Tap* (1984) ... Don't lose another minute; watch it today!

Mind Management

By this point in our voyage, we've examined management through multiple lenses. This bonus chapter approaches the subject from yet another angle—possibly the most difficult—how we manage our brain.

Acquiring new skills and techniques, such as those presented throughout this book, requires changing behavior. It's not easy crushing to bits previous habits and building up bright, shiny new ones in their place. On top of this Olympian effort is the fact that the most ingrained behaviors are invisible to the naked eye . . . habits of the mind.

Our beliefs define us, affecting our behavior. Recall this revelation from chapter 4:

> **Your sole areas of direct responsibility are**
> **your thoughts, your words, and your actions.**

If I am convinced that I add little value as a manager (thoughts), my behavior (words and actions) will reinforce my belief. Interactions are the concretization of our thoughts.

How we manage is ultimately a reflection of our thoughts.

Changing your thoughts about management changes you as a manager.

What if you decide to pretend (or even believe) your staff are your teachers—especially those who challenge you? What if you want to get a handle on each lesson they are here to teach you? What if you reframe your expectations to support the idea that they won't change to suit your whims? Consider this:

- No one will change until you do.
- The behavior of others mirrors your own thinking coming back to you.

Revising your perspective is for *yourself;* this isn't about letting other people off the hook.

Jumpin' Thru Hoops

Mind Management

Changing your thoughts alters your actions. If you tend to blame other people and external circumstances for your moods, attitudes, and behaviors, try this exercise.

Not certain if you do? Ask yourself whether any of the following sound familiar.

- It's his fault I . . .
- I gave up because she . . .
- If I had a better team, I could . . .
- If it weren't for all the changes around here, I would have . . .
- Once there is new management, I will . . .
- If only I had enough time, I could . . .

Now conduct a self-assessment of your thought habits.

Select a three-hour block during the course of a workday during which you anticipate engaging in normal activities. This can include lunch or breaks, meetings, or any slice of work life. During this time, log your thoughts in the chart below, in half-hour increments. You will not be able to capture every thought that passes through your head; just use this opportunity to increase your consciousness of the thought patterns that occupy prime real estate in your mind.

Fill in the first two columns during the three hours of internal observation. The third and final column will be filled in later.

Time	What are my thoughts?	Are my thoughts primarily inner-directed (toward myself) or outer-directed (toward others)?	Are these thoughts primarily positive or primarily negative?
1:00–1:30			
1:30–2:00			

Jumpin' Thru Hoops (continued)

2:00–2:30			
2:30–3:00			
3:00–3:30			
3:30–4:00			

At the end of the time period, fill in the third column, assessing your thoughts in each row as essentially positive or essentially negative. Then answer the following:

My primary thought habits focused on:_____

My energy is most frequently directed ( ) internally or ( ) externally

I was most surprised by:_____

I would like to redirect my thought habits to be more:_____

I would like to redirect my thought habits to be less:_____

An area to work on:_____

Generalizing, Deleting, and Distorting

Neuro-linguistic programming (NLP) is a cognitive science focused on improving rapport and communication through an increased, conscious use of the two primary ways people communicate—neurologically (kinesthetic) and linguistically (language). That's pretty heady. Don't fret. I can break it down into bite-sized pieces. I've snuck in bits and pieces of NLP throughout this book, similar to a cookbook recipe that sneaks veggies in on unsuspecting carnivores. It's good for you, even if you don't realize what's going on behind the scenes.

Since we've made this far, I'll come clean. This section is very NLP.

GENERALIZATIONS

Generalizations occur when a single experience comes to represent an entire category of situations.

Generalizations can be helpful guides at times. Examples of useful generalizations include:

- Always proof a memo before distribution.
- Exercise caution when crossing the street.
- Think clearly before clicking Send.

Yet, unchecked generalizations can limit effectiveness:

- Never back down in a negotiation; it is a sure sign of weakness.
- Never trust anyone.
- Only thinkers can handle tough business decisions.
- Feelers always know the best way to keep a team together.

Generalizations are dangerous because past events can inordinately influence current experience and future expectations.

Models are helpful if they are assessed and evaluated for usefulness. Taken to an extreme, however, generalizations lead to a flat interpretation of the world, such as "Nobody appreciates me around here" or "Everyone ignores my ideas."

Remember, generalizations are *never* true . . . except right now.

Certain red-flag language leads to generalizations:

Everyone	Impossible	May not	Always	Never
No one	Must	Should	Can't	Doesn't
Nothing	Nobody	Every time	If . . . then	Causes
Whatever	None	Everything	Whenever	_____ (add your own)

Notice red-flag language in your head and conversations. Arguments bring out the best in red flag language:

- You *never* listen to me!

- *Every time* I speak, you interrupt!

- You *always* have to be right.

- *Whatever* I say, you disregard.

- *Whenever* we go somewhere, you lose your temper.

- You do that *all the time.*

- She *never* pays attention to me.

- He gets the credit for what I do, *every time.*

- People *should* greet others when they see them at work.

Love those.

The frequency with which many of us use generalizations is downright startling. In case you're interested, generalizations are also called universal quantifiers. If you *were* interested, you might want to consider a hobby . . . or NLP.

DELETIONS

Selectively attending to certain aspects of experience while excluding others is called deletion. Like generalizations, deletions serve a fine purpose in the right context. Recall the last time you were in a room where several conversations were transpiring simultaneously—perhaps a boardroom before a meeting, a networking event, or a department lunch. Your ability to filter out extraneous sounds and focus on your immediate conversation served you well in this context. Deletion enables us to render our sensory intake into manageable, relevant chunks.

The flip side is that an overly active filter prevents us from recognizing important data such as creative solutions to challenges, nontraditional resources, or exemplary behavior from a difficult staff person.

Thinkers may err in the direction of deleting subtle nonverbal cues sent out during a performance appraisal or negotiation, for instance. Feelers can get derailed in the same situations when they pick up on a strong emotion, such as confusion or anger from another party, causing feelers to miss important verbal cues.

Being aware of your propensity for deletion in charged situations can mitigate their impact.

DISTORTIONS

One example of distortion is the visualization of an event prior to the actual experience. Athletes frequently cite visualization prior to an important race or competition as a factor in success. Those in healing professions claim measurable increases in health when traditional methods of wellness are combined with guided imagery.

Distortion creates shifts in experience of sensory data. Artists, scientists, and fiction writers use the gift of distortion to come up with new concepts and original theories. Much advancement and beauty owes its beginnings to distortion of accepted reality.

Like generalization and deletion, however, unchecked distortion has a downside. Distortion can lead to innovation; it can also limit the richness of one's experience. Distortion can block the intake of novel experiences.

Many misunderstandings owe their roots to distortions of reality. My supervisor might pass by my office and give a perfunctory nod. I can distort this to mean he is irritated with the report I turned in last night and is working on a way to restructure the department sans my position. Yet his reality could have been that he was preoccupied with his next meeting, where he has to persuade a new client to purchase several thousand units of product. Perhaps my report is crucial to his success and was tucked under his arm as he hurried past.

Distortions can prevent us from experiencing events as positive, because false beliefs weigh us down.

Small Acts, Big Impact

On a recent business trip, I happened into conversation with a Southwest Airlines flight attendant, Tara. She was a new hire who intended to stay with the company, as she put it, "for life." Tara was remarkably effusive about Southwest. This kind of instant loyalty is rare among employees of large corporations.

Tara proceeded to enthusiastically inform me about how much senior management cares about the flight crews. To illustrate her point, she gave this example: Upon conclusion of each flight, the crew is responsible for tidying up the aircraft and preparing it for incoming passengers. All staff on board—except the pilots, who have their own preparations to make—are expected to contribute.

Recently a Southwest vice president was on board Tara's flight for company business. Upon the flight's conclusion, the VP stayed on board after the other passengers disembarked, got up, and helped clean the cabin with the regular crew. His action—which took about ten minutes—lives on not only in the minds of the crew present but also in all the others who have by now heard the story.

Do you think that VP was a T or an F? What's your gut response?

Chances are if you're a T, you guessed T, and Fs guessed F. That is because temperament explains reasons behind behavior as much as the behavior itself. The same behavior could have distinct motives.

Both Ts and Fs value the behavior of this VP and so identify him as being one of their own . . . for different reasons. His actions were practical and efficient—if he himself is a T, he probably helped out because it was quick, easy, builds collateral, and seemed like the right thing to do. If the VP is an F, he did it because it was a friendly gesture, made him feel good, enabled him to bond with the flight attendants, and showed that he doesn't pull rank.

This little ditty personifies so much of what we've discussed on these pages. Real impact is made without being "bossy." Managers are always being watched. A lasting positive impression requires much more than exuding what is typically considered "charisma."

Little acts on the part of management add up to major, positive effects on the larger business. In 2010, 140,000 people applied for 140 jobs at Southwest. For the mathematically challenged, that means a measly 0.1 percent of the applicants received job offers. Retention is the highest in the industry. Customer satisfaction also is the highest in the industry.

And how are Southwest's interviewers instructed to make hiring decisions? They are told to select candidates based on evidence of a "customer service mentality." Southwest ranks people skills above technical skills in importance during interviews. Southwest believes people can learn the nuts and bolts of their jobs once they're on board.

Except, I hope, the pilots. Somebody ask them about that.

Southwest believes happy people make generous, warm employees who will go the extra mile for each other and the customers. This approach is a mix of T and F. On a practical, thinker level, Southwest leadership recognizes that if the company shows that it values employees, such as by paying above industry standards, the employees will go further for the company too. Plus, Southwest saves millions through a high retention rate. And for the feelers? Employees are encouraged to send each other "LUV Letters" to acknowledge each other for jobs well done. Something for everyone. Employees are made to feel they matter and are appreciated.

How can you incorporate T and F incentives for your team?

Paying Attention Pays Off

From 1927 through 1932 a series of experiments began at Western Electric's Hawthorne Works in Cicero, Illinois. The Hawthorne study was designed to examine the effect of factors such as light and humidity levels on worker productivity.

The researchers were surprised by a major, unexpected finding: Productivity improved *regardless* of experimental manipulation of external factors. Effectiveness increased merely from the psychological stimulus of being observed. The implications of these findings are thrilling! Okay, I get excited easily.

A major outcome of this research—which was intended only to examine physical settings in the workplace—was that social group influences and interpersonal factors must be considered even when performing efficiency research such as time-motion studies. In the decades since, the Hawthorne effect has provided the rationale for untold human relations theories and practices.

Conclusions of the Hawthorne study include:

- The quality of relationships between managers and employees influences how effectively employees carry out assignments.
- Individual aptitude is an imperfect predictor of job performance.
- Even when physical and mental potential is indicated, production is strongly influenced by social factors.
- Informal networks and norms, such as systemic definitions of a fair day's work, influence productivity.
- The workplace is a social system composed of interdependent parts.
- The act of merely observing people changes them.

It is not possible to observe without affecting the observed, challenging basic beliefs about objective measurement.

Cue *Twilight Zone* music. I'm so into this.

This goes further. What the Hawthorne folks discovered complements physics research proving quantum interconnectedness.

According to quantum theory, thoughts and experience are related. There is no truly objective external reality; the physical universe does not exist independently of an observer's thoughts. As physicists have discovered, no objects—or people for that matter—have well-defined boundaries. Not only do atoms not have clear boundaries, they are not even present as particles until we observe them. Physicists have proven—or more accurately, have discovered—that atoms spread out continuously in wave form until they are observed. So, is an atom a particle or a wave? Experimentation led to an unexpected discovery: It depends.

This mind-blowing discovery threw the scientific world into uncharted territory. Unobserved atoms behave like waves; observed atoms exhibit patterns of particles.

A wave is fluid and indicates possibility; it cannot be measured at a single point in space and time. A particle collapses that infinite possibility into one measurable, observable reality. An observer transforms the wave into a single particle through the act of observation.

This now-established principle links back to the Hawthorne effect. The Hawthorne study demonstrated—in an entirely different arena— merely paying attention, giving people (or atoms) your attention, has an impact on their behavior.

Taking It Home . . . or Rather, to Work

How does this cool stuff relate to you as manager? You don't have to be infallible to be a plenty good manager. You don't have to be brilliant. And you don't have to possess supernatural powers to distinguish Ts from Fs with razor-sharp accuracy.

Just making an effort at the most fundamental level will yield positive results. Paying more attention to your direct reports, in and of itself, not only can ramp up their productivity but also shows your interest in their success. Applying one or two new techniques from this book is icing on the cake. There is plenty of margin for error.

 Flex!

Manage your mind-set, pay attention to the people around you, seize opportunities to perform small acts that make a big impact . . . and start to discover the enjoyable part of being a manager.

P.S. The system with the most flexibility exerts the greatest influence.

Signing Off:
You're STILL Here?

With the best leaders, when the work is done, the task accomplished,

the people will say, "We have done this ourselves."

—Lao Tzu

And so, my friends, it has come to this.

This is pretty much a wrap. I'm getting that misty-eyed last-day-of-camp feeling. Which proves that pouring a healthy dose of T into an F doesn't change the core temperament.

I'm wiped out. You can take things over from here. I'll back up just about any management hypothesis you espouse at this late hour.

Speaking of which, let's talk about what happens when you release control. In my experience, despite complaints about having much to do, letting go is one of the scariest feats for a manager.

One of my favorite team problem-solving activities involves a challenge with a Koosh ball, an all-time great invention if you ask me (no one has asked me yet, so it feels good to get my opinion out there). Without going into all the details, I'll tell you that the team's task is to figure out how to get the Koosh ball to travel through the hands of every participant as fast as humanly possible.

Most teams I work with eventually achieve the stated objective. I consider less than one second as fast as humanly possible for teams of eight to twenty people. Don't you?

I'm not going to tell you the whole rigmarole, because if you find yourself in one of my programs you'll be tempted to be a big show-off.

The point (one of several, actually) is that teams can only accomplish the task as fast as humanly possible by surrendering control of the Koosh ball. Rather than passing the ball from hand to hand, the team needs to figure out a way for the ball to roll of its own accord, letting gravity take over. Getting out of the way (chapter 1) becomes a metaphor for the value of relinquishing control. This generally goes over quite well with your employees, particularly when they know you'll support them as needed.

At a certain point, you just have to get out of the way.

Instincts! Or . . . What If I Screw It All Up?

Let's discuss that gut of yours. Would it kill you to do a few sit-ups? Just kidding. You're gorgeous as is. What I'm really interested in is your inner gut. (Forget that inner child; he just riles things up.) Befriending your inner gut can do wonders for your management style, decision-making ability, and confidence.

Modern times don't give the gut its due.

Technology permeates our lives and can be used to weigh options, provide heaps of data for "logical" choices, and just about everything else. And yet . . .

Guts are low tech. You can use them on takeoff and landing. The gut instinct is a subtle messenger, requiring us to temporarily exit the chaotic din of our hectic lives to hear what our intuition has to say. Many people are too distracted, impatient, or frazzled to bother.

This is an error.

Your gut—call it intuition, sixth sense, or instinct—is a gold mine of wise decisions, choices, and actions. Why do so many managers disregard or suppress it?

You're asking me? I've no idea. Disregarding a free, accurate, travel-ready resource makes no sense. Inquire around and let me know what you find out. It'll be fun to poke holes in the arguments for why ignoring intuition is a sound leadership practice.

In my book (this one, to be precise), dissing instincts flies in the face of being successful. We must be the strongest version of ourselves to climb past the plateaus and up to that coveted management pinnacle. And the road map to the path up is way deep inside your core. I love the following quote from a decidedly unsentimental, very T, retired U.S. Navy captain:

> "The more you trust yourself and your instincts,
> the better manager you'll be."

I've been so adamant. Here's a caveat. Check instincts against facts and account for the input of others. I had the unfortunate experience of working with a manager who held his intuition in singular regard above all else. No data was checked; he did what he sensed was right, even when his direct reports provided compelling cases for why another path was better and all exterior information shouted the opposite truth. He needlessly derailed his career at breakneck speed.

And now I will share a humiliating true story that I can't believe I'm putting into print. Too many late nights, I suppose. You need to be a very loyal reader for the right to peruse this story. If you haven't already, go read everything else I've ever written. Make it snappy; I don't have all day. Also, if you're recklessly skipping around in this book, happening upon this story randomly, that doesn't count. You need to have read your way this far for me to expose myself in this way.

Okay, then! Now that you've demonstrated your overall commitment and support, I will allow you to continue reading.

This event occurred at the U.S. Space and Rocket Center in Huntsville, Alabama. USSRC is NASA's first visitor center. It opened in 1970 and has hosted more than 12 million visitors on expansive grounds chock-full of real rockets, an impressive museum, and a multifaceted educational center. I was a leader-in-training for a team-building program and having a blast. In the following activity, I was a regular participant.

The stakes for success were sickeningly high. Get this: If we didn't locate our lost-in-space fellow astronaut within thirty minutes, he would be *permanently* lost in space. They gave us no information, however, about where this astronaut might be hanging out. I can say those facilitators had a real gift for making everything seem urgent and real. My partner in crime and I looked at each other frantically. Spontaneously, side by side, we began running as fast as our legs could carry us. After a sizable sprint, the facilitators caught up to us, huffing and puffing.

"Wait! Wait! Where are you going?" they asked. My teammate and I looked at each other, mortified. We had no idea where we were headed.

Until that charming moment, I may have denied that my take-action impulse could so override my create-a-strategy business school training. Suddenly I realized how easy it is to "just do it" without thinking through things for a split second.

Participating in this enlightening experience cemented for me the value of discussing before doing. And yet . . . ! If I had merely attended a lecture on the value of strategic planning compared to reactionary leadership, I would have zoned out. How pedestrian! How obvious! Instead, experiencing firsthand my own authentic and frankly ineffective natural response to a challenge was something I couldn't skim over. I was forced to face an aspect of my style that needed attention. Noticing my reactive tendencies enables me to modify them to best match circumstances. Sometimes fast action works; other times it needs to be calibrated.

The same can be said for thinker and feeler reactions. Sometimes we respond to adversity best in a pragmatic, calm, disassociated manner. Sometimes we do better letting empathy lead. Other times a mix is most effective.

You're in charge, so grab the reins and make a grand entrance on your own terms. It's the only way to go.

Here's a joke I heard years ago; it stuck. Two construction workers are sitting on a high beam way up in a building site, preparing for their lunch break. One opens his lunch box and says, "Tuna again! I hate tuna." His buddy responds, "Why don't you ask your wife to make you something else then?" To which the first worker grumbles, "I make my own lunches."

Are you him? Fix yourself up a management sandwich that fits you. Why suffer needlessly?

From Me to You: A Closing Gift

Although reproduction of sections of this book must be cleared through my publisher (see opening pages), I grant you permission to adapt and use any of the activities described in these pages. It's an infinite pie out there; savor your favorite slice.

My writing goals are to help improve work life, relationships, productivity, and your satisfaction as a manager. Enjoy!

Tell me your stories.

One last assignment before we part ways:

Be fabulous.

Oh, wait. You already are. Check!

See you again soon . . . Time to clock out.

Notes

1. Norton Juster, *The Phantom Tollbooth* (New York: Random House, 1961), 213.

2. Isabel Briggs Myers, Mary H. McCaulley, Naomi L. Quenk, and Allen L. Hammer, *MBTI Manual: A Guide to the Development and Use of the Myers–Briggs Type Indicator,* 3rd ed. (Mountain View, CA: Consulting Psychologists Press, 2003).

3. Anne Lamott, *Bird by Bird: Some Instructions on Writing and Life* (New York: Anchor Books, 1995), 18.

4. Victor Frankl, *Man's Search for Meaning* (New York: Perseus, 2000).

5. Pauline Rose Clance, *The Impostor Phenomenon: Overcoming the Fear that Haunts Your Success* (Atlanta: Peachtree Publishers, 1985).

6. Norton Juster, *The Phantom Tollbooth* (New York: Random House, 1961), 165–170.

7. Rahel Schwartz, *Working Conditions and Secondary Traumatic Stress* (New York: Yeshiva University, 2008).

8. *Entrepreneur,* February 2007, 84.

9. Carl Jung, *Memories, Dreams, Reflections* (New York: Random House, 1961), 247.

10. Devora Zack, *Networking for People Who Hate Networking* (San Francisco: Berrett-Koehler, 2010), 77.

11. Ibid., 22, 36.

12. Cited in Gregory Berns, *Satisfaction: The Science of Finding True Fulfillment* (New York: Henry Holt and Company, 2005).

13. Ibid.

Relevant Reads

"Classic." A book which people praise and don't read.
—Mark Twain

Adams, Marilee. *Change Your Questions, Change Your Life: 10 Powerful Tools for Life and Work*. San Francisco: Berrett-Koehler, 2009.

Bandler, R., and J. Grinder. *Reframing: Neuro-Linguistic Programming and the Transformation of Meaning*. Salt Lake City: Real People Press, 1982.

Biech, Elaine, ed. *Trainer's Warehouse Book of Games: Fun and Energizing Ways to Enhance Learning*. San Francisco: Pfeiffer, 2008.

Cameron, Julia. *The Artist's Way Every Day: A Year of Creative Living*. New York: Penguin, 2009.

Covey, Stephen, A. Roger Merrill, and Rebecca R. Merrill. *First Things First: Coping with the Ever-Increasing Demands of the Workplace*. New York: Simon & Schuster, 1994.

Csikszentmihalyi, Mihaly. *Flow: The Psychology of Optimal Experience*. New York: Harper Perennial, 2008.

Doty, Elizabeth. *The Compromise Trap: How to Thrive at Work without Selling Your Soul.* San Francisco: Berrett-Koehler, 2009.

Drucker, Peter. *Managing the Nonprofit Organization.* New York: Harper, 1990.

Fisher, R., and D. Shapiro. *Beyond Reason: Using Emotions as You Negotiate.* New York: Penguin, 2005.

Fisher, R., and W. Ury. *Getting to Yes: Negotiating Agreement without Giving In.* New York: Penguin, 1983.

Gladwell, Malcolm. *Blink: The Power of Thinking without Thinking.* New York: Little, Brown, 2005.

Goleman, Daniel. *Destructive Emotions.* New York: Bantam Dell, 2003.

Hare, Robert. *Without Conscience: The Disturbing World of the Psychopaths among Us.* New York: The Guilford Press, 1999.

Howard, Pierce. *The Owner's Manual for the Brain: Everyday Applications from Mind-Brain Research.* Austin, TX: Bard Press, 1994.

Kador, John. *Effective Apology: Mending Fences, Building Bridges, and Restoring Trust.* San Francisco: Berrett-Koehler, 2009.

Kahnweiler, Jennifer. *The Introverted Leader: Building on Your Quiet Strength.* San Francisco: Berrett-Koehler, 2009.

Katie, Byron. *Loving What Is: Four Questions that Can Change Your Life.* New York: Three Rivers Press, 2002.

Kaye, Beverly, and Sharon Jordan-Evans. *Love 'Em or Lose 'Em: Getting Good People to Stay.* 4th ed. San Francisco: Berrett-Koehler, 2008.

Knight, Sue. *NLP at Work: The Essence of Excellence.* London: Nicholas Brealey Publishing, 1995.

Kroeger, Otto, and Janet Thuesen. *Type Talk at Work: How the 16 Personality Types Determine Your Success on the Job.* New York: Dell, 1993.

LeDoux, Joseph. *The Emotional Brain: The Mysterious Underpinnings of Emotional Life.* New York: Touchstone, 1996.

O'Connor, Joseph, and John Seymour. *Introducing NLP: Psychological Skills for Understanding and Influencing People.* London: HarperCollins, 1995.

Perkins, Dennis N. T. *Leading at the Edge: Leadership Lessons from the Extraordinary Saga of Shackleton's Antarctic Expedition.* New York: 2000.

Pink, Daniel. *A Whole New Mind: Moving from the Information Age to the Conceptual Age.* New York: Penguin, 2005.

Rosenblum, Noah. *Be the Hero: Three Powerful Ways to Overcome Challenges in Work and Life.* San Francisco: Berrett-Koehler, 2009.

Rosenbluth, Hal. *The Customer Comes Second.* New York: William Morrow, 1992.

Rosenstein, Bruce. *Living in More than One World: How Peter Drucker's Wisdom Can Inspire and Transform Your Life.* San Francisco: Berrett-Koehler, 2009.

Russo, J. Edward, and P. J. H. Schoemaker. *Winning Decisions: Getting It Right the First Time.* New York: Random House, 2002.

Senge, Peter. *The Fifth Discipline: The Art and Practice of the Learning Organization.* New York: Doubleday, 2006.

Society for Neuroscience. *Brain Facts: A Primer on the Brain and Nervous System.* Toronto, Canada: Society for Neuroscience, 2006.

Stout, Martha. *The Sociopath Next Door.* New York: Three Rivers Press, 2006.

Ventrice, Cindy. *Make Their Day!: Employee Recognition that Works.* 2nd ed. San Francisco: Berrett-Koehler, 2009.

Wheatley, Margaret. *Leadership and the New Science: Discovering Order in a Chaotic World.* San Francisco: Berrett-Koehler, 2006.

Zack, Devora. *Networking for People Who Hate Networking.* San Francisco: Berrett-Koehler, 2010.

Acknowledgments

The deepest principle in human nature is the craving to be appreciated.

—William James

A gigantic THANK YOU! to . . .

Neal (my exceptional editor) and Jeevan (my illustrious illustrator) for providing priceless raw material for this book through your daily interactions, talking me down from panic attacks, and providing continual support. Neal, thanks for your guidance, peaceful demeanor, and patience. Jeevan, besides everything else, I'm so glad you know how to draw elephants.

My Writers Salon and BK community of friends and supporters. The exceptional support from Arielle, Bonnie, Catherine, Courtney, Cynthia, David, Diane, Dianne, Ginger, Johanna, Katie, Kathy, Kristen, Kylah, Maria Jesus, Marina, Michael, Rick, Zoe, and Steve. My first-rate reviewers and editors Katherine Armstrong, Christopher Morris, Josh O'Conner, and Todd Manza. Last and first, James Killian, who taught me that only brownies and roasts are done; everything else is finished.

My tireless, generous, obstinate, and fiercely loyal airlift. You're busier than anyone else and still make the time.

I would not be the person I am without my three sweet and tender hooligans. Thank you for encouraging and supporting me as I write. You're superstars.

Thank you to my clients who gave generously of your time and stories. You took surveys, shared experiences, and provided insightful unattributed quotes throughout this book.

I will stop here, before I start questioning my own meager contributions to this project.

Index

About Only Connect Consulting, Inc.

Only connect!
—E. M. Forster, *Howards End*

Devora Zack is president and founder of the leadership development firm Only Connect Consulting, Inc. OCC has grown annually as a 100 percent referral-based business with more than one hundred clients on the roster. Services include keynotes, seminars, assessments, consulting, and executive coaching. Sample clients include:

- **Australian Institute of Management**
- **CapGemini**
- **Cornell University**
- **Deloitte**
- **Federal Aviation Authority (FAA)**
- **John Deere**
- **London Business School**
- **Mensa International**
- **National Association for Women Business Owners**
- **National Association of Personal Financial Advisors**
- **National Institutes of Health (NIH)**
- **Ohio State Law School**
- **SAIC**
- **Smithsonian**
- **Transportation Security Administration (TSA)**
- **Treasury Executive Institute**

- **U.S. Department of Education**
- **U.S. Department of Energy**
- **U.S. Patent and Trademark Office**
- **Urban Land Institute**

OCC specializes in leadership, team building, networking, management, presentation skills, communication, focus groups, change, creative problem solving, strategic plans, stress and time management, business theater, customer service, negotiation, Myers–Briggs Type Indicator, and 360-degree feedback.

For inquiries and bookings contact:
connect@myonlyconnect.com
www.onlyconnectconsulting.com

Author Trivia

I was working on the proof of one of my poems all the morning,

and took out a comma. In the afternoon I put it back again.

—Oscar Wilde

In case you haven't put together the pieces, I'm Devora. I like my name because it means "to speak kind words," something I aspire to do amidst my propensity to poke fun at anyone in my path. I'm a bit of a wreck in real life, though I keep up a solid front as a writer and consultant. (If you don't believe me, contact Jeevan at Berrett-Koehler and ask him. He has nothing better to do; don't hesitate to give him a ring.) I'm also pretty clumsy.

When I'm not writing, my favorite pastimes include complaining about writing deadlines, reminding my sons they exist to serve me, force-feeding friends and family, tap dancing from time to time, working out to manage my excess energy, causing trouble, and reading anything that makes me laugh.

I've been a visiting faculty member at Cornell University's Johnson Graduate School of Business for more than fifteen years, teaching management skills and networking to MBA students from all over the world.

On my office wall is a Cornell MBA, University of Pennsylvania BA, Phi Beta Kappa membership, USDA woman-owned business award, and Myers–Briggs Type Indicator and Neuro-Linguistic Programming certifications. None of the frames match.

I've been quoted and featured in, for example, the *Wall Street Journal, USA Today, Forbes,* Oprah.com, Fox News, *British Airways, Cosmo International, CEO, CIO,* and a range of media in Africa, Asia, Australia, and Europe. My first book, *Networking for People Who Hate Networking,* has been translated into ten languages at the time of this book's publication.

I am fortunate to love my work as a leadership consultant, author, and speaker. I also dig fan mail, so keep that in mind for a rainy day.

Any further questions, your honor?

THE ASTD MISSION:

Through exceptional learning and performance, we create a world that works better.

The American Society for Training & Development provides world-class professional development opportunities, content, networking, and resources for workplace learning and performance professionals.

Dedicated to helping members increase their relevance, enhance their skills, and align learning to business results, ASTD sets the standard for best practices within the profession.

The society is recognized for shaping global discussions on workforce development and providing the tools to demonstrate the impact of learning on the organizational bottom line. ASTD represents the profession's interests to corporate executives, policy makers, academic leaders, small business owners, and consultants through world-class content, convening opportunities, professional development, and awards and recognition.

Resources
- *T+D (Training + Development)* Magazine
- ASTD Press
- Industry Newsletters
- Research and Benchmarking
- Representation to Policy Makers

Networking
- Local Chapters
- Online Communities
- ASTD Connect
- Benchmarking Forum
- Learning Executives Network

Professional Development
- Certificate Programs
- Conferences and Workshops
- Online Learning
- CPLP™ Certification Through the ASTD Certification Institute
- Career Center and Job Bank

Awards and Best Practices
- ASTD BEST Awards
- Excellence in Practice Awards
- E-Learning Courseware Certification (ECC) Through the ASTD Certification Institute

Learn more about ASTD at www.astd.org.
1.800.628.2783 (U.S.) or 1.703.683.8100
customercare@astd.org

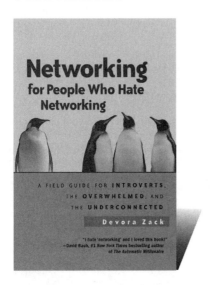

Berrett–Koehler
Publishers

A community dedicated to creating
a world that works for all

Visit Our Website: www.bkconnection.com

Read book excerpts, see author videos and Internet movies, read our
authors' blogs, join discussion groups, download book apps, find out about
the BK Affiliate Network, browse subject-area libraries of books, get special
discounts, and more!

Subscribe to Our Free E-Newsletter, the *BK Communiqué*

Be the first to hear about new publications, special discount offers, exclusive articles, news about bestsellers, and more! Get on the list for our free
e-newsletter by going to **www.bkconnection.com**.

Get Quantity Discounts

Berrett-Koehler books are available at quantity discounts for orders of ten or
more copies. Please call us toll-free at (800) 929-2929 or email us at **bkp
.orders@aidcvt.com**.

Join the BK Community

BKcommunity.com is a virtual meeting place where people from around
the world can engage with kindred spirits to create a world that works for
all. BKcommunity.com members may create their own profiles, blog, start
and participate in forums and discussion groups, post photos and videos,
answer surveys, announce and register for upcoming events, and chat with
others online in real time. Please join the conversation!

MIX
Paper from
responsible sources
FSC® C012752
www.fsc.org

Certified
Corporation
bcorporation.net